Margaret H. Bonham

Soft Coated Wheaten Terriers

Everything About Selection, Care,
Nutrition, Behavior, and Training

BARRON'S

CONTENTS

UNDERSTANDING THE SOFT COATED WHEATEN TERRIER

Today the Wheaten enjoys its status as a companion dog. Gone are the days when it hunted vermin around the Irish farms and helped its master pursue quarry. The Soft Coated Wheaten Terrier is as comfortable on the couch beside its family members as it once was on the misty hills of the Emerald Isle.

Meeting a Friend for Life

What is so special about the Soft Coated Wheaten Terrier? When you first see one, perhaps you are drawn to the striking wheaten open coat that gives this dog its name, or perhaps it is its mild manner or its outgoing disposition. Later, as you become more familiar with the breed, your viewpoint tends to shift from looking at a dog to looking at an individual. You find yourself treating the Wheaten more as a member of your family than as a family pet. Such is the power of the Soft Coated Wheaten Terrier. Wheaten breeders are fanatical in their devotion to this jovial breed, and this overwhelming devotion is returned tenfold by the Wheatens themselves.

The Soft Coated Wheaten Terrier is a happy, friendly dog of medium height and weight. Although the American Kennel Club (AKC) classifies it as a terrier breed, the Wheaten generally has a milder temperament and is less "scrappy" than most of its terrier cousins. Its roots are deep and steeped in Irish tradition, but it is not the dog of nobility. It is the dog of the common Irishman, the farmer, the herder, and the huntsman who needed a hardy dog to fill many roles.

Today the Wheaten enjoys its status as a companion dog. Gone are the days when it hunted vermin around the Irish farms and helped its master pursue quarry. The Soft Coated Wheaten Terrier is as comfortable

on the couch beside its family members as it once was on the misty hills of the Emerald Isle. If you open your home to a Soft Coated Wheaten Terrier, these dogs will open their hearts to you.

A Leprechaun in Disguise

The Soft Coated Wheaten Terrier is the Peter Pan dog of the terrier breeds. Always looking for something new and exciting, always happy and jovial, it is the dog that simply will not grow up. With warm and friendly personalities—and impish humor—one can imagine Wheatens as leprechauns in disguise. Wheatens

constantly delight and frustrate their owners with new antics. Like small children, they love and trust everyone and will go home with the nearest stranger as easily as going home with you. Wheatens make poor kennel dogs, requiring constant human interaction.

Although they have mild and less aggressive temperaments, Wheatens can best be described as "active." They enjoy being in the center of activity at all times, and if there is nothing going on, they will come up with something to do. If it is not something you have planned, they will plan it. In fact, mischief could be their middle name.

General Positive and Negative Traits

A common Wheaten trait is jumping straight up and kissing a person on the face in a heartfelt welcome. Wheatens will greet both strangers and longtime friends in this manner. An exuberant Wheaten, however, can knock down small children and muddy good clothing in little time. It is difficult to train a Wheaten not to do this, but it can be done if started early and if the dog is consistently trained not to jump up.

Wheatens are not outdoor dogs. Although they enjoy the outdoors, their beautiful coat becomes a magnet for twigs, leaves, and dirt. A Wheaton's coat will quickly mat, even if groomed meticulously. Snow sticks to it in huge clumps, and rain quickly tangles and mats the hair. These are high-maintenance dogs, requiring frequent combing and brushing, not to mention trimming.

Wheatens are not great obedience dogs. They bore easily with repetitious commands and require a lot of "fun time" to keep training enjoyable. Off-leash obedience work is often confounded when the Wheaten discovers something far more interesting and runs off to investigate. As a result, many Wheatens have embarrassed their owners at obedience trials. **Caution:** Never let a Wheaten off leash in an unfenced area as its curiosity may lead it too

far away; these dogs may also bolt through open doors and into traffic.

Wheatens are very sensitive dogs and empathize with an owner's moods. They do not take punishment well. They love to be with their owners and love to explore new things. Wheatens are good with sensitive and gentle children but, as with all dogs, should never be left alone with a toddler or small child. In addition, they make good watchdogs, barking at ringing doorbells and the neighborhood dog as it walks by, but they do not guard. They are more likely to greet a burglar with an enthusiastic kiss than with a growl.

You may hear that Wheatens are the hypoallergenic breed of the dog world. This statement is not completely true. Though Wheatens do

not shed, their dander, oils, and saliva may cause allergic reactions in sensitive individuals.

A Brief History of the Soft Coated Wheaten Terrier

The Early Irish Terriers

The Soft Coated Wheaten Terrier shares a common lineage with its cousins, the Irish Terrier and the Kerry Blue Terrier. Although the nobility in Ireland kept Irish Wolfhounds and other hunting and coursing dogs, they forbade the commoner such privileges; the Irish farmer instead bred medium-sized terriers as farm dogs. These versatile dogs killed vermin, herded livestock, hunted quarry to ground, and alerted farmers to intruders.

One romantic legend claims that after the Spanish Armada's defeat, a single blue-gray dog swam ashore and bred with the native Irish wheaten-colored dogs, producing the Kerry Blue, a cousin to the Soft Coated Wheaten Terrier. Some claim the dog that swam to shore was a Portuguese Water Dog. Regardless of the legend's validity, both wheaten and blue terriers appeared in nineteenth-century dog shows as "Irish Terriers."

The Irish Coat Versus the American Coat

The American version of the Soft Coated Wheaten Terrier has a fuller and thicker coat than its Irish counterpart. The Irish coat is generally less "puffy," with a brilliant shine, and requires less maintenance than the American coat. There is some controversy surrounding the introduction of the Irish coat into American stock, but many breeders regard this as a

necessity to preserve the breed in its current standard.

Descriptions of some of these early terriers included open or soft coats as well as the better-known wiry, dense coats.

The Soft Coated Wheaten Terrier Becomes Its Own Breed

Although the Soft Coated Wheaten Terrier has its roots in the Irish and Kerry Blue terriers, the Wheaten was not recognized by the Irish Kennel Club until 1937. (The English Kennel Club recognized the Irish Terrier in 1880 and the Irish Kennel Club recognized the Kerry Blue in 1922.) Indeed, the Wheaten may not have become a recognized breed at all had it not been for the efforts of Dr. G. J. Pierse, a Kerry Blue breeder, who recognized the outstanding qualities of the Wheatens. Two breed clubs, the Irish Terrier and the Glen of Imaal Terrier breed clubs, opposed the Wheaten Irish Terrier becoming a breed. Only when Dr. Pierse changed the name of the breed to the Soft Coated Wheaten Terrier were both clubs mollified. The English Kennel Club recognized the Wheaten in 1943.

Some of Dr. Pierse's dogs became the foundation stock of Maureen Holmes, the famed author of The Wheaten Years: The History of Ireland's Soft Coated Wheaten Terrier. Mrs. Holmes's dogs dominated in Ireland at one time, and her lines still influence the Soft Coated Wheaten Terrier today.

The Soft Coated Wheaten Terrier in America

Seven Soft Coated Wheaten Terrier puppies arrived in Boston on November 24, 1946. These were the first Soft Coated Wheaten Terriers in America. Miss Lydia Vogel, of Springfield, Massachusetts, owned two of these dogs and proceeded to show and produce Wheatens in the United States. However, real interest in the breed did not develop until breeders O'Connors and Arnolds imported dogs from Ireland in 1957.

The Soft Coated Wheaten Terrier Club of America (SCWTCA) formed in 1962 on St. Patrick's Day. Its founding members included the O'Connors, the Arnolds, the Mallorys, and the Wurzbergers. On March 17, 1973, the Soft Coated Wheaten Terrier achieved AKC recognition.

CHOOSING A SOFT COATED WHEATEN TERRIER

Most people prefer to purchase a puppy rather than an adult dog. There are several valid reasons for this. With a puppy, you start with a "clean slate": A new puppy has not yet learned any bad habits, it is ready for training, and it is very impressionable and will bond readily to you. However, raising a puppy takes much time and energy.

Are You Ready to Own a Soft Coated Wheaten Terrier?

Choosing a Wheaten—or any dog, for that matter—is a decision that should not be taken lightly. Many dogs, including Wheatens, end up in animal shelters because their owners were not willing to take responsibility for their pets. Take this test to determine if you are ready to own a Wheaten:

✔ A healthy Wheaten will live on average ten to fifteen years; are you able to rearrange your lifestyle to accommodate an animal that is dependent solely on you?

✔ The cost of a puppy does not end at its purchase price. Your Wheaten Terrier will require ongoing food and veterinary expenses throughout its life. Puppies and elderly Wheaten Terriers will generally incur more expenses than adults. Can you financially afford to care for your pet?

✔ Does everyone in the household want a Wheaten Terrier, or any dog, for that matter? All members of the family must agree on a new pet.

✔ Who will take care of the Wheaten? Children cannot always be depended on to take care of a live animal; the Wheaten must be the responsibility of an adult in the household.

✔ Do you have a fenced-in backyard that is dig proof, climb proof, and jump proof? Wheatens, as terriers, have a tendency to dig.

✔ Are you willing to take your Wheaten for a daily walk?

✔ Are you willing to go to obedience classes to train and socialize a puppy?

✔ Are you able to leave your Wheaten Terrier alone for no more than nine hours at a time?

✔ Are you able to give your Wheaten attention every day?

✔ Are you willing to put up with muddy paw prints on your clothing? Wheatens love to jump up and kiss their owners. This habit is very difficult to break.

✔ Is anyone allergic to dogs in your family? Though Wheatens generally do not shed and are considered good dogs for those who have allergies, some people are still allergic to their dander or saliva.

✔ Are you willing to devote time to brushing your Wheaten several times a week and trimming it often? Wheatens are high-maintenance dogs that require frequent grooming.

✔ Are you able to tolerate the destructiveness associated with a dog? Puppies and dogs may chew the wrong things. You may find a hole in your garden where your Wheaten has excavated a new tunnel. Puppies don't come housebroken and the adult dog may have an occasional accident.

If you can truthfully answer each of these questions positively, then you are ready to purchase your Wheaten.

Questions and Answers

1. *Question:* Are Soft Coated Wheaten Terriers good with children?

Answer: Soft Coated Wheaten Terriers are easygoing by nature and will generally get along with considerate children; however,

no dog should ever be left alone with a small child. In addition, Wheatens are known to jump up on people and may, in their enthusiasm, knock down small children. Also, any dog may bite, given provocation, and even a medium-sized dog such as a Wheaten can do a considerable amount of damage. Wheatens that are not properly trained and socialized or that are the result of poor breeding may behave unpredictably.

2. *Question:* Are Soft Coated Wheaten Terriers good watchdogs?

Answer: Soft Coated Wheaten Terriers will bark to alert you if something unusual is happening, but they make poor guard dogs as they consider everyone their friend.

3. *Question:* How time-intensive is it to groom a Soft Coated Wheaten Terrier?

Answer: Soft Coated Wheaten Terriers require frequent brushing and trimming. Because their coats do not shed, like double-coated breeds, they require trimming to keep their coats from growing too long. Their coats will mat without combing, so brushing at least three times a week is necessary. *As a Wheaten matures from its puppy coat to its adult coat (usually around 12 to 18 months) you may notice that the coat will mat more easily*

than usual. This period requires more frequent brushing than at other times in their lives.

4. *Question:* Are Soft Coated Wheaten Terriers easy to train?

Answer: Soft Coated Wheaten Terriers are smart dogs, but due to their terrier nature, they can be stubborn and independent at times. You will find that your Wheaten will learn commands easily and then ignore them when he does not feel like obeying. If you are looking for an obedience OTCH Champion, you should not choose a Wheaten.

5. *Question:* I am allergic to dogs. I heard that Soft Coated Wheaten Terriers are hypoallergenic. Is that true?

Answer: Wheatens do not shed the way double-coated breeds do, although some dead hair does come out while brushing them. Some people who are allergic to dogs find that they can tolerate Wheatens; however, the allergic reaction largely depends on the person. Some people are allergic to dog saliva, rather than the dog hair and dander. If you are allergic to dogs, it might be best to spend a few hours at a Wheaten breeder's kennel to determine whether or not you can tolerate a Wheaten Terrier.

6. *Question:* Do Soft Coated Wheaten Terriers require much exercise?

Answer: Wheatens are moderately active dogs and enjoy playing with their owners. They require daily walks and some exercise in the backyard but are able to adjust to your schedule. The Wheaten is not a dog to leave out in the yard all day and does not need the intensive exercise some breeds require.

Puppy or Adult?

Most people prefer to purchase a puppy rather than an adult dog. There are several valid reasons for this. With a puppy, you start with a "clean slate": A new puppy has not yet learned any bad habits, it is ready for training, and it is very impressionable and will bond readily to you. However, raising a puppy takes much time and energy.

If there is no one to socialize, train, and watch over a puppy during the daytime, consider purchasing or adopting an older Wheaten Terrier (see page 22, "Buying an Adult Wheaten").

Older Wheatens will usually bond to their new owners as quickly as a puppy would, and many older dogs are housebroken and may know some commands. If a more mature and older Wheaten suits your lifestyle better than a puppy, then choose an older Wheaten. Try to find out as much as you can about the dog before you commit to purchasing or adopting it. Some dogs may have learned bad habits that you may have to break or that may require more of your time and effort than you have to commit. Be honest with yourself when deciding (or not deciding) on one. Still, there are many loving adults, both in rescue and from breeders, that are ready to be your faithful companion.

Male or Female?

Each Wheaten will have its own temperament, regardless of sex. Males may be more willing to please you, and females may be a little more independent, but these are generalities. Temperaments vary between dogs. Choose the gender of your Wheaten based on your personal preference and your breeder's recommendations. If you have another dog, it might be wise to choose a puppy or dog of the opposite sex. While male and female dogs do fight, there is generally less aggression between the sexes than between two males or two females.

Show or Pet Quality?

If you are looking for a wonderful family member, a good friend, and an exercise companion, a pet-quality Wheaten Terrier is for you.

If you are looking to show your Wheaten in AKC shows and breed litters of outstanding puppies, then purchase a show-quality Wheaten. However, you should be aware that show-quality puppies usually cost much more than pet-quality puppies, and many breeders

will not sell show-quality puppies to first-time Wheaten owners. Some breeders may have clauses in contracts requiring that the owners show the dog.

Does this mean that the pet-quality Wheaten is inferior to the show-quality Wheaten? Absolutely not! Show quality simply means that the puppy conforms closer to the Soft Coated Wheaten Terrier standard than other dogs. A pet-quality puppy may be a little too big or too small according to the standard, may have an incorrect bite, or may not have a correct coat. The reason most pet-quality Wheaten Terriers are pet quality is merely cosmetic—you may not even notice it—and does not affect the ability of the Wheaten to become a wonderful addition to your family.

Pet-quality puppies cost less than show-quality puppies because most breeders wish to offer a companion at a reasonable price. Reputable breeders require pet-quality puppies to be neutered or spayed because they do not wish the undesirable cosmetic trait to be passed into future generations of Wheaten puppies.

Buying a Puppy

Many dog owners purchase a puppy on impulse. Wheaten puppies, however cute, should not be considered impulse items, as they are a ten- to fifteen-year investment. Puppies quickly become dogs and lose their "cuteness." All Wheaten puppies are adorable, no matter where they come from. When you buy a puppy from a reputable Wheaten breeder, you have more than just a puppy; you have a puppy with a guarantee that it will be free of hereditary diseases. And it is important to know that all reputable breeders will take the dog back anytime in the dog's life, should it be a puppy or a five-year-old adult.

Genetic Problems

Almost all breeds now have genetic problems such as hip dysplasia and progressive retinal atrophy (PRA). Although the Wheaten Terrier is generally a very healthy breed, the breeder should have had the parents certified. Renal dysplasia (RD) and PLE/PLN are three genetic conditions in the Soft Coated Wheaten Terrier that can be fatal (see pages 57–58 for more information on RD and PLE/PLN).

Do not just accept statements such as "he's had his hips and eyes checked" or "he doesn't have any genetic diseases." Ask for proof. OFA (from the Orthopedic Foundation for Animals) and CERF (from the Canine Eye Registration Foundation) are the two certifications; ask to see the original documents, not photocopies. Hip dysplasia is a crippling and painful genetic disease that may cost thousands of dollars to surgically correct. PRA and other eye problems can lead to blindness. Wheatens with RD often die before they turn three years old. Did the breeder have a veterinarian perform an ultrasound and a urine test? Ask to see the results.

Breeders

Contact the Soft Coated Wheaten Terrier Club of America, the national breed club for Wheatens, to obtain a list of Wheaten breeders in your area. You can obtain addresses and phone numbers from the AKC (see page 92).

After you have obtained a list of names of breeders from a valid source, contact each breeder and ask some tough questions. The breeder, if he or she is reputable, will also be asking you questions. Plan a visit to look at the kennel facilities, meet the dogs, and determine whether a dog or puppy from the breeder's lines suits your needs. One thing to keep in mind: With the exception of a dam, who may be protective of her puppies, any dog in the breeder's kennel should be approachable. If the breeder is uncomfortable with you petting a dog, you may want to reconsider buying from that breeder. Aggression and timidity are major faults in Wheatens.

Too often, the buyer is more concerned over whether the breeder is "a nice person." "Nice people" are also known to run puppy mills, dump puppies into animal shelters, and breed dysplastic dogs. Puppy mill owners and backyard breeders are going to act "nice," because they want you to buy their puppies. On the other hand, a reputable breeder may not seem nice because he or she is asking tough questions. The breeder asks tough questions because he or she cares about the Wheaten puppies being sold. A breeder will often turn down ready buyers in order to find the best homes for the puppies. This breeder will ask questions about you, your family, and your

home. These questions may seem intrusive, but it is a sign that the breeder really cares about the new home his or her Wheaten puppy may be going to.

Finding a Reputable Breeder

✔ Does the breeder have only one or two breeds that he or she breeds? Reputable breeders focus on one or two breeds to improve the standard.

✔ Does the breeder belong to the Soft Coated Wheaten Terrier Club of America or to a local club? Wheaten breeders will be involved in the local breed clubs.

✔ Do the puppies' parents have conformation, obedience, or agility titles? A quality Wheaten should have or be working toward a title. If the parents are not titled, how close are they to obtaining titles?

✔ How did the breeder choose the stud dog? Was it a dog he or she had on hand, or did the breeder search for the right dog to breed to his or her own female? The breeder should not have bred his or her female to what was available, but rather looked for a dog that would improve the conformation and bloodline of the stock.

✔ Can the breeder provide photographs and information concerning the parents, grandparents, great-grandparents, uncles, aunts, and cousins of the puppies? If he or she cannot tell you about these dogs, then how is the breeder able to breed a quality Soft Coated Wheaten Terrier?

✔ Does the breeder have OFA and CERF certifications on both parents? A Wheaten's hips should be at least a Good rating, preferably Excellent. The CERF certification rating is either Passed or Failed. Ask to see the original certificates if the breeder has both parents. If the breeder has only the female, ask to see the original certificate of hers and a photocopy from the male's owner.

✔ Has a veterinarian cleared the parents of RD and PLE/PLN? Has a veterinarian tested the puppies for RD?

✔ Why did the breeder breed these two Wheatens? The answer should be to produce puppies that will improve the Soft Coated Wheaten Terrier breed. Often, the breeder will keep one or two puppies to see if they will turn out to be show prospects, but occasionally the breeder will not keep a puppy because it did not turn out the way he or she thought it may. Never buy a Wheaten puppy from someone who is breeding dogs to make a profit. Do not buy a puppy from someone who breeds dogs to be just like his or her pet. The breeder should be striving to improve the breed, not breed pet-quality puppies.

✔ Ask the breeder for a contract. The contract is your bill of sale; the AKC papers are not a bill of sale. If the breeder does not have a contract, look for your puppy elsewhere. The breeder should stipulate that he or she will take the Wheaten back under any condition.

The breeder should also guarantee the puppy free from illnesses, parasites, and hereditary defects. The breeder will stipulate that you must adequately care for the puppy and will require that you never allow your Wheaten puppy to run at large. The contract should not have stud rights or requirements for breeding unless this is something you have agreed to. The guarantee should not have a caveat such as strange diets or extreme limitation of exercise.

✔ Reputable breeders will not press you to buy a puppy. They will first try to educate you about what it means to own a Soft Coated Wheaten Terrier. They will tell you about the good points and the shortcomings of the breed. They may ask for references. Do not be insulted if a breeder sounds like he or she is grilling you. The breeder wants to be absolutely certain that this Soft Coated Wheaten Terrier puppy will fit in with your family and your particular situation. If the breeder tells you "there's only one left, you better buy it," don't. There are other litters from reputable breeders.

✔ How old are the puppy's parents? Neither parent should be bred before it is two years old. They cannot have their OFA certification until that time. Breeding a Wheaten female before two years of age is cruel—the female Wheaten is not ready emotionally or physically until two years of age.

✔ How long has the breeder been involved with Wheatens? Backyard breeders are usually new at breeding Wheatens, but occasionally you will find someone reputable who has his or her first litter of puppies, but who is also very involved in showing Wheatens.

✔ When have the puppies been wormed and vaccinated? A reputable breeder will either worm the puppies or have a veterinarian perform a fecal analysis on the puppies to determine if worms are present. Puppies should have received their first vaccinations at five to six weeks of age.

✔ When is the earliest the breeder will allow you to take a puppy? The youngest a Wheaten puppy should leave his mother is at eight weeks old—no exceptions! The puppy must spend time with his mother and littermates to properly socialize him with other dogs. Before this time, the puppy may be very insecure and stunted in his emotional development.

✔ What items will the breeder provide when you are ready to take your Wheaten home? The breeder should provide you with: information on raising and training a Wheaten, the puppy contract, the AKC puppy papers, copies of the parents' OFA and CERF certifications, a sample of the puppy food the breeder has been feeding the puppies, a record of vaccinations and worming, a vaccination schedule, a pedigree, and any other information he or she thinks might be useful to a new Wheaten puppy owner. Some breeders may include a toy to help ease the puppy into his new home.

Be sure to ask for references. The breeder should be able to provide you with names and phone numbers of other members of the Soft Coated Wheaten Terrier Club of America or of local clubs and people who have bought puppies who will gladly vouch for this breeder.

Buying an Adult Wheaten

Buying an older Wheaten is much like purchasing a puppy; you should also purchase your older dog from a reputable breeder. Sometimes breeders have an older puppy or adult that has not turned out the way they had hoped for showing and are looking to find a good home for this dog. Many times, the cost of these older dogs is lower because most people are looking for puppies. Use the same guidelines in searching for a reputable breeder as you would use for buying a puppy.

Shelters and Rescues

Sadly, some Wheaten Terriers are dumped in shelters and dog pounds by owners who did not understand the level of commitment necessary to own a dog. These dogs may be perfectly good pets, waiting for someone with the patience and love necessary to train them.

The rescued Wheaten's background is unknown, as is his health record, but if you are willing to take that chance, in time and with patient training, a rescued Wheaten can make a loving pet. Be certain that when you do adopt such a dog, there is a clause in the adoption that states you can return the dog if a veterinarian finds the dog to be sick or unsound. Then take your new Wheaten to the veterinarian for a full physical examination, including fecal tests (for worms) and a hip X-ray. If your Wheaten is older than two years, your veterinarian can tell you if he has hip dysplasia. Worms can be cured; hip dysplasia cannot.

Contact the Soft Coated Wheaten Terrier Club of America (see page 92 for the address) for a list of Wheaten rescue organizations near you.

The "Puppy Papers" or AKC Registration

All purebred AKC dogs have AKC registration, the proof that your Wheaten is a registered purebred. It does not mean that your Wheaten is somehow very valuable or more valuable than anyone else's. It does not mean your Wheaten is show quality. It does not mean your Wheaten is healthy or well bred.

Breeders refer to the Puppy Papers as "blue slips." On one, you will find a place to fill in your Wheaten's name and your name, as well as a place where both you and the breeder must sign to indicate a transfer of ownership. The AKC now has a check box that the breeder may check if the puppy is to have a limited registration. If checked, this means that the puppy may not ever be bred and cannot have its litters registered under the AKC. In this way, a reputable breeder may indicate that the puppy is being sold to a pet home only. When you receive the registration back, it will have stripes on it, indicating that the dog is never to be bred.

Do not misunderstand: Just because you have the Puppy Papers, does not mean your puppy is registered. It is not. You must fill out the appropriate boxes and send the form into the AKC along with the registration fee. Do not confuse the pedigree with the registration. The pedigree is the puppy's family tree. It may look very impressive with dogs that have strange registered names and the authentic AKC gold seal, but again it is not a sign of quality, nor does it register your puppy to you.

If you are buying an adult Wheaten, be certain that the breeder transfers over the registration papers as well. Depending on whether or not the dog is deemed show quality, the papers may either be a full registration or a limited registration. The breeder must sign the registration form to indicate a transfer of ownership. You must then sign the form and return it to the AKC with the appropriate transfer fees.

These papers, however impressive, do not constitute a bill of sale. They are not a contract between you and the breeder. If the breeder does not have a contract drawn up and intends to only use the AKC registration papers, you may want to reconsider buying a puppy or dog from this breeder.

Breeder Contracts

Before you even look at a litter of Wheaten puppies and fall hopelessly in love with them, you should ask for the breeder's contract. The contract should be anywhere from two to four pages long, stipulating the terms of the sale. Should you read the contract and not understand it, have an attorney look it over. Check out the following:

1. The contract should have a guarantee that the puppy or dog is free from genetic diseases and is healthy. Most breeders require the owner to take the puppy to the veterinarian between twenty-four to seventy-two hours after purchase to confirm the puppy's health. Guarantees for hip dysplasia and eye problems may have a time limit of two to five years and may have certain exclusions such as whether the owner bred the Wheaten before she was two years old. The breeder will usually refund all or part of the puppy's purchase price or provide a suitable replacement should a veterinarian find a problem.

2. The contract should have what is called either "Right of First Refusal" or "First Right of Refusal." This means that if the new owner no longer wants the dog, he or she must first contact the breeder before selling or giving away the Wheaten to any other party. All reputable breeders will take back the dog they sold.

3. The contract will require that you take adequate care of your Wheaten. You may be required to have a fenced-in yard or a kennel, and the breeder may require that you not allow your Wheaten to roam.

4. If the puppy is sold as a pet, you may have to spay or neuter her before she reaches six months of age.

5. If the puppy is show quality, you may be required to obtain OFA and CERF certification before breeding.

6. The contract should not have anything that limits your ownership of the puppy. You should never be forced into co-owning a dog, especially if you are paying a fair amount of money.

7. You should not be required to breed your Wheaten nor to owe a puppy from some future

litter back to the breeder. This is unfair to you; you should not have to provide stock to this breeder, especially if you want a pet and not a show dog.

8. Finally, the guarantees should not have clauses that stipulate that the contracts will not be honored unless certain unusual conditions are fulfilled. Any conditions on the guarantees should be reasonable and not include such things as bizarre homemade diets or limiting the amount of sensible exercise.

Choosing a Puppy from the Litter

When you are about to select a puppy, the first thing you should do is to observe them. Are there any that are shy or timid? Is there a scrappy bully among the group? Is there one that doesn't show any interest in you, but instead wanders around looking to get into mischief? Is there one that is interested in your presence and happy to be petted?

You do not want a shy or timid puppy because she will most likely be shy or timid for the rest of her life. You do not want a scrappy Wheaten because she will be headstrong and difficult to train. You do not want an independent wanderer who will not listen to your commands. You want a puppy that is interested in you. Often, the puppy that comes to you first may be too dominant, so do not be fooled into thinking that this puppy chose you. Instead, watch how the puppies interact. That will give you a good clue as to their personalities.

With the breeder's permission, separate each puppy you are considering from the litter and observe her reactions as you pet and cuddle her. At this point, the dam may become nervous or overly protective, and the breeder may have to separate her from the puppies in order for you to perform your tests. Ask the breeder to do so if he or she does not.

Testing the Puppy

✔ Look at the puppies. Are they clean, bright-eyed, and well cared for? Are they alert and attentive? You may have awakened them from a nap, but they should still respond well to you. If the puppies act lethargic or cry piteously, you should perhaps consider another

litter. Anything unusual, such as distended bellies, might indicate a problem.

✔ One puppy will no doubt be your favorite. Pick her up and snap your fingers behind her head. She should turn and look or at least respond. Wave a toy in front of her face and see if the puppy will try to grab it. While these tests are not perfect, they will help identify a deaf or blind puppy.

✔ Pick up the puppy and cuddle her. A normal reaction to being held and cuddled individually might be a little apprehension followed by cheerful acceptance.

✔ Gently place the puppy on her back and hold her there. She may struggle or yip for a few moments and then quiet down as you rub her tummy.

✔ If the puppy reacts aggressively by either trying to nip or struggling violently, let the puppy go. This puppy is very dominant and may be difficult for you to train.

✔ If the puppy cries and submissively urinates, the puppy is too submissive and timid.

✔ You can further test a puppy by rolling a ball or tossing a toy. The puppy should go after it eagerly and play, not shy submissively away from it or ignore it. Puppies have short attention spans so you may have to throw the object a few times before you get the puppy's attention. Clap your hands and call to the puppies. They should come over to investigate.

Choosing an Adult Wheaten Terrier

Choosing an adult Wheaten is different from choosing a puppy. A puppy is full of unknowns and surprises as he grows up; the adult is pretty much what you will see when you

choose him. However, you should be choosing an adult that will have a stable personality.

✔ The adult Wheaten should be outgoing and friendly. Avoid any timid or aggressive Wheatens.

✔ The Wheaten may be exuberant but should not be hyper when greeting you.

✔ If the Wheaten knows commands, walk him on a leash and practice the commands. Offer him a dog biscuit whenever he performs the command correctly.

✔ Call the Wheaten to you by clapping your hands. He should come readily at the sound of a friendly voice.

✔ Watch for any unusual behavior; if the Wheaten behaves in a different way than you expect, you may have to look elsewhere.

Questions for the Breeder About the Adult Wheaten

✔ Ask the breeder if the Wheaten is house-broken, crate trained, and obedience trained.

✔ Find out from the breeder what bad habits the Wheaten has, if any.

✔ Ask the breeder why the Wheaten is available. If the dog is a returned animal, ask the breeder why he was returned.

✔ Ask for the name and phone number of the former owners and talk with them, if this is practical. Ask them why they returned the dog. They may be candid and tell you more about the dog you are considering than the breeder was able to.

Note: Do not be put off if the older Wheaten you have chosen has a name you do not like. You can rename the dog after you have brought him home; just be certain to stay with the name you have chosen so as not to confuse your new dog.

BRINGING YOUR SOFT COATED WHEATEN TERRIER HOME

Before you bring your Wheaten puppy or adult home, you must first decide where she will sleep and spend most of her time. If you simply must have an outside dog, reconsider your decision about purchasing a Soft Coated Wheaten Terrier. Though they are hardy dogs, they really belong inside with you.

What to Expect of Your New Wheaten

Puppies are adorable, but like all babies, they require attention. A puppy must be cared for, taught, and loved; she is not a toy that you can put away when you have finished playing with her. Be ready for the following:

• Sleepless nights from the puppy crying because you took her away from her mother.
• Waking up at 2 A.M. because the puppy has to go out.
• Missing lunch because you have to rush home from work or school to let the puppy out.
• Coming straight home from work or school because you have to walk the puppy.
• Chewed shoes, plants, books, furniture, carpet, and sheetrock.
• Realizing that nothing on the floor is safe anymore.
• Soiled carpet; if your carpet is white or some other light shade, expect to replace it with a darker color that will not show stains as readily.
• Having to feed the puppy three times daily and walk her once a day.
• Brushing out your Wheaten's coat daily.
• Arranging to care for your Wheaten if you go on vacation.

Wheatens require attention, love, and training, as well as vaccinations and regular veterinary checkups.

Where Will Your Wheaten Stay?

Before you bring your Wheaten puppy or adult home, you must first decide where she will sleep and spend most of her time. Wheatens are people dogs and will be unhappy if you leave them outside and away from their family. They may show their displeasure by nuisance barking, digging holes, or escaping. If you simply must have an outside dog, reconsider your decision about purchasing a Soft Coated Wheaten Terrier. Though they are hardy dogs, they really belong inside with you.

Note: In order to avoid the rather impersonal "he/she," the name "Rusty" will be used throughout the remaining chapters.

Running at Large

When you let Rusty outside, you should not simply turn him out to run at large. Wheatens are notorious for running away and will go home with anyone. Responsible dog owners contain their dog in either a fenced-in backyard or a kennel run that is escape proof. Dogs that run at large are a nuisance. They get into the neighbor's garbage, chase and kill wildlife, and may get run over by traffic. The city and suburbs are not safe places for a dog to run loose. Even in the country, there are

Household Hazards

Item	Hazard	Action
Children's toys	May cause obstructions or choking.	Keep toys out of reach.
Laundry	May cause an obstruction if swallowed.	Keep laundry out of reach.
Coins	Coins, especially pennies, may be swallowed, causing zinc or "penny" poisoning.	Keep coins out of your Wheaten's reach.
Household plants	May be poisonous.	Remove plants to a safer area. Do not use in areas where your Wheaten goes.
Pesticides/poisons	Highly toxic.	Keep out of reach.
Electrical cords	May cause electrocution if chewed.	Hide electrical cords; use specially designed extension cords that "sense" if the cord has been chewed through.
Antifreeze, windshield-washer fluids in garage	Extremely poisonous.	Keep your Wheaten out of the garage.
Deicer for sidewalks	Caustic.	Use a pet-safe deicer.
Household cleaners	Poisonous.	Use children-safe latches on drawers and cupboards.
Glass tables, knickknacks	Can cut your Wheaten if broken.	Remove items out of your Wheaten's reach.
Toothpaste, medicines	Poisonous.	Keep out of reach.
Landscape plants	May be poisonous.	Keep your Wheaten away from landscape plants, or plant only nontoxic varieties.
Landscape gravel	May cause obstruction if swallowed.	Keep your Wheaten away from landscape gravel.
Garbage pails	Your Wheaten may raid and eat items from it; may poison your Wheaten.	Put garbage pail in a cupboard under the sink; keep your Wheaten out of the bathroom.

many dangers for your Wheaten. Coyotes and mountain lions kill loose pets frequently, and farmers will often shoot strays that menace their expensive livestock. Dogs will run in packs and kill valuable game animals, forcing wildlife rangers to shoot the dogs.

Fences and Kennel Runs

If you can afford to fence in your backyard, do so. It should be a sturdy fence that is dig proof, jump proof, and climb proof. A 6-foot (1.8-m) fence offers the best protection.

Many people are unable or unwilling to fence in their property. This provides some unique problems for the pet owner. The best alternative to a fenced-in backyard is a kennel run. Kennel runs are relatively low in cost ($100 to $300), compared to fencing in an entire front yard or backyard. They do not have to take up much room and provide a secure outdoor place when you cannot exercise your Wheaten.

Electronic invisible fences keep a dog contained within your property boundaries, pro-

vided that you have trained him to do so, but they do not protect him from loose dogs or from other dangers encroaching on your yard. The electronic invisible fences lose their effectiveness when the collar's battery dies or if Rusty discovers that he will not receive any more shocks once he leaves the boundaries. This containment method has its drawbacks, as you must first train the dog to respect the property line. You cannot install it and just turn him loose; otherwise, it will be ineffectual. These electronic invisible fences work best when there is someone at home who can train and periodically watch the dog.

Cables and Chains

Never leave your Wheaten tied up on a cable or chain; Rusty can quickly become tangled and severely injured. Dogs left alone on a chain frequently become frustrated and aggressive. Stray dogs can attack your Wheaten, and children can tease him.

Leaving Your Dog Unsupervised: Leaving any dog outside unsupervised is not a good idea. A lonely dog will bark and annoy your neighbors, causing them to call animal control and file complaints; neighborhood bullies will pick on your dog and tease him; unscrupulous people who have a dislike for dogs may poison your Wheaten; dog thieves look for pets for dogfighting and baiting aggressive dogs or for selling to an underground market for research. Do not leave your Wheaten outside while you are not at home.

Your Bedroom

Rusty will bond more closely to you if you put his bed in your bedroom. This provides eight hours or more time you are spending with him, even though you are sleeping, and will also help reduce his separation anxiety. However, Rusty should have his own bed, preferably in his own crate (see page 40 for a discussion about crates). There are several reasons for this, mostly dominance oriented. You need to establish now that humans are the masters over dogs. You will help avoid possible dominance problems by enforcing Rusty's sleeping area early on. Train him that beds are human territory only.

When Rusty cries for the first couple of nights, you can tap the crate and tell him to be quiet—all from the comfort of your own bed. If you are a light sleeper, you are unlikely to get much sleep the first few nights while both you and Rusty adjust to the new arrangements.

Puppy- and Dog-Proofing Your Home

Puppies and dogs find many things in the home extremely enticing. Use the Household

CHECKLIST

First Year's Cost of a Soft Coated Wheaten Terrier Puppy

The following is a cost breakdown of ownership of a healthy Wheaten Terrier puppy during the first year. Be aware that illnesses and accidents can substantially increase this amount. These numbers are estimates only.

✔ Veterinary exam: $15 to $45.
✔ Vaccinations:
  • Three sets of DHCPP, averaging $30 to $60 per vaccination.
  • Two sets of bordetella vaccinations, averaging $20 to $30 per vaccination: optional unless the puppy is exposed to kennel situations or large numbers of dogs.
  • Two sets of Lyme disease vaccinations, averaging $30 to $60 per vaccination; necessary in Lyme areas.
  • One rabies vaccination; averaging $10 to $30.
✔ Worming:
  • Puppy wormings: $20 to $50.
  • Heartworm test: $20 to $50.
  • Heartworm medication, one year: $75 to $200.
✔ Spay or neuter: $75 to $200.
✔ Puppy food, one year, approximately one 40-pound (18-kg) bag per month: $300 to $720, depending on the food.
✔ Dog crate: $75 to $250.
✔ Miscellaneous leashes, collars, toys: $100 to $200.
✔ Grooming equipment: $100 to $500.
✔ Visits to the groomer: $40 to $100 each.

Hazards table to check if your house is safe for your newest family member.

Other items such as newspapers, boots, shoes, and draperies may prove enticing to your Wheaten, and though they might not be poisonous, you may not want them chewed on. Always provide the appropriate toys and chewing items for your Wheaten so Rusty will be less willing to chew something else (see below).

Teething and Chewing: All puppies teethe and chew; even adult Wheatens chew to keep their teeth clean and their gums healthy. Chewing is a natural instinct. You should provide suitable chew toys for your Wheaten, including large, hard rubber toys, heavy rope toys, nylon toys impregnated with flavors, and hard knuckle- or marrowbones. Rawhide and

TIP

Chewing Distractions

Here are some ideas for providing chewing distractions:

✔ Take a hollowed-out marrowbone and fill it with peanut butter.

✔ Fill hollowed-out solid rubber "indestructible" toys with hot dogs or bits of meat.

✔ Give your dog rawhide, cow hooves, pigs' ears, smoked knucklebones.

✔ Offer nylon bones.

✔ Provide "puzzle toys" that allow you to hide treats inside.

cow hooves make good chew items, but can come off in large pieces and be swallowed. Your main concern should be whether or not the item will cause an obstruction. Watch your Wheaten puppy as he chews a particular toy. If the pup manages to take it apart in large chunks that can be swallowed, take the item away.

• Never give Rusty chicken, turkey, fish, or steak bones; they are sharp and splinter easily and can perforate an intestine.

• Soft latex toys are also dangerous, as Rusty can tear them apart and swallow the pieces. Keep in mind Rusty's chewing habits as you buy toys and treats. If you are not sure, purchase the most indestructible items and watch him as he chews them.

• Never let Rusty chew on clothes items such as old socks, pantyhose, slippers, or shoes. Do not allow him to chew on bedding or towels. You may not care about that particular item, but he will have trouble distinguishing between the old worn-out sneaker and your $200 pair of dress shoes.

When you find Rusty chewing something that you have not designated as a toy, tell him "No chew!" and take away the item while offering something suitable to chew in return. Some people like to use the word "Trade!" You can say "No chew, Rusty! Trade!" and offer a toy or food for the item. Most Wheatens will gladly relinquish their prize if the item offered is more appealing (more on training begins on page 45).

A Good Veterinarian

Choose a veterinarian before you purchase your Wheaten. A good veterinarian is well known throughout the dog-owner community. Ask your Wheaten's breeder or other Wheaten owners for the name of a good veterinarian in your area. If they do not know any in your area, ask a dog-owning neighbor. If you are not satisfied with your options, you may have to consider looking up nearby veterinarians in the local Yellow Pages or obtain a list of practices from the American Veterinary Medical Association.

Once you have limited your search to two or three veterinarians, call them and make appointments to visit them. If you drop by unannounced, you may show up during a busy time when the veterinarian may not have time to talk with you. When you make an appointment, ask for a tour. The clinic should reflect the veterinarian's personality. Is it clean and well organized? Is the staff pleasant and courteous? Do you feel comfortable leaving your pet there? Ask to see the cages and boarding kennels, if the veterinarian does any boarding.

Are the cages large enough for the animals housed? Are the runs escape proof? Are they clean?

Ask the veterinarian about hours, both normal and emergency. Many veterinarians are on call for emergencies. If your veterinarian does not handle off-hour emergencies, you will have to bring your Wheaten to an emergency animal clinic, which can be quite costly.

Finally, you should like the veterinarian. If you do not like him or her, you may not follow all his or her instructions, which may compromise your Wheaten's health.

Bringing Your Wheaten to the Veterinarian

Take Rusty to the veterinarian for a full checkup before you bring him home. Bring any health and vaccination records the breeder or former owner provided. Your veterinarian may ask for a stool sample before your appointment. Collect the stool sample in a plastic bag and bring it with you.

When you give the veterinarian the stool sample and health records, he or she will most likely want to run a fecal analysis to check for internal parasites. If you have an older Wheaten and live in a heartworm state, the veterinarian may suggest a heartworm test and suggest that you put your Wheaten on a heartworm preventative. If your Wheaten's

T I P

Protecting Your Puppy

It is important that you protect your young Wheaten puppy from deadly contagious diseases. Although socialization is very important for your Wheaten puppy, take extra care during the first sixteen weeks of his life to prevent exposure to strange dogs and diseases. Diseases such as parvovirus and distemper can infect a young puppy even if he has had his shots.

vaccinations are not up to date, or if it is time for your Wheaten puppy's next series, the veterinarian will want to vaccinate your Wheaten, and should examine your Wheaten for signs of disease.

Follow your veterinarian's advice concerning vaccinations. There are serious contagious diseases that puppies have no resistance to, such as parvovirus and distemper. The mortality rates for these diseases are 50 percent or higher (for more on vaccinations, see page 60).

You should also follow your veterinarian's advice concerning worms and heartworm (discussed more fully on page 62). Worms will make your puppy sick, and in many cases will cause malnourishment or even death, if left untreated. Heartworm is a deadly parasite that attacks the heart and pulmonary arteries. It is transmitted through a mosquito's bite. Once contracted, it is very expensive to treat heartworm, which is potentially life-threatening.

Should your new Wheaten prove to be unhealthy, contact the breeder immediately. If you bought your Wheaten from a reputable breeder, the breeder may offer to pay your veterinary expenses, offer a replacement, or refund your money.

Bringing Your Wheaten Home

Schedule some time off from work or school so you can spend more time with your new pet. Your Wheaten will adjust quicker to family life if you spend more time with him. If you cannot take time off, pick up your Wheaten on a Friday night so you will have the weekend to spend with him.

The Car Ride Home

When you pick up your Wheaten from the breeder, bring a travel crate to transport him to the veterinarian and then home. If you do not, Rusty may get agitated or carsick and interfere with your driving. Do not put Rusty in a cardboard box or other container where he can climb or chew his way out. Even if you bring another person along to handle him while you drive, you should transport him in a crate.

Introducing Your Wheaten to Other Pets

Other Dogs

Wheatens are very outgoing and friendly and most can tolerate other dogs well. Still, there may be problems introducing your Wheaten to another pet. If you have another dog, the other dog may look on the new Wheaten as an interloper and may behave in unexpected

ways including snarling and biting. Never bring a new dog home and leave him alone with your current dog. This could lead to a serious dogfight.

You may wish to reconsider purchasing a Wheaten if your current dog is much bigger than the Wheaten or usually shows aggression toward other dogs. Some dogs and breeds are naturally inclined toward aggression and fighting. If this is true of your other dog, that tendency will always be there, regardless of training or correction. Do not leave your Wheaten unsupervised with this type of dog; he may be severely injured or killed. A much larger dog will outmatch your Wheaten if a dogfight ensues. The choice is yours: Many large dogs are gentle and nonaggressive, but, as previously stated, regardless of whether or not you think your current dog will be friendly with your new Wheaten, never leave them together unsupervised.

Have a family member or friend bring your current dog on leash to a park and wait for you to bring Rusty there. Bring Rusty to the park on leash and introduce them. Watch for signs of aggression: walking stiff-legged, hackles raised—when the hairs on the back of the neck and shoulders stand up—hard stares, lifting or curling the lip, growling or snarling. One thing to be careful of is to not hold the leash too tightly the first time you introduce the two dogs. You will telegraph your nervous feelings to your dogs, and they will pick up on it and become nervous as well.

Assuming the first introduction goes well, you should still not put the two together unsupervised for a while; there will be some sorting out to do as the dogs figure out their own "pecking order." Give the dogs equal affection;

do not neglect your current dog because you have a new one. If your other dog acts aggressively toward your Wheaten or vice versa, seek the help of a professional dog behaviorist or trainer.

Wait until after your Wheaten has received his final series of vaccinations before taking him to training classes, pet supply stores, boarding kennels, and dog parks. Do not allow strange people to pet your Wheaten puppy without washing their hands, and do not allow your Wheaten puppy to step through or smell strange dogs' excrement. You can further prevent tracking in parvovirus by mixing a spray bottle of one part chlorine bleach and 22 parts water and spraying it on the bottom of your shoes when you enter your home.

Cats

Introducing Rusty to the Family Cat: Your cat may hiss and scratch at the new addition, so be ready to keep Rusty from pouncing on the cat or chasing it. Correct any chasing or other aggressive behavior. While the Wheaten is not as scrappy as some terrier breeds, it is still a terrier and may chase the cat. Do not leave the Wheaten and the cat alone together. Eventually, Rusty may learn to ignore the cat and find other things more interesting.

Other Pets

Never leave birds, rabbits, mice or other rodents, or reptiles alone with the Wheaten. Do not introduce them, or your small pets may suffer. Again, Wheatens are terriers and terriers were bred to kill vermin. Your other pets may be too tempting for your Wheaten. Keep your pocket pets in a safe place away from your Wheaten.

═══ T I P ═══

Keeping Your Wheaten Puppy Quiet at Night

Some trainers recommend using a hot water bottle and an old-fashioned alarm clock to keep the new puppy quiet. The warmth from the hot water bottle is supposed to simulate your Wheaten's littermates, while the ticking of the alarm clock is supposed to simulate the rhythm of the mother's heart.

The First Few Hours and Nights

By now you should have chosen a place for Rusty to sleep and dog-proofed your home. When you bring him home, he should be naturally curious to investigate his new surroundings, but first let him relieve himself outside. In the excitement, this may take awhile, but be patient; your Wheaten, especially a puppy, will eventually have to relieve himself. Then bring him inside to explore.

Do not let the other family members swarm over your new addition; they may frighten him. Let each person quietly introduce himself or herself to Rusty with a pat or a treat. He may naturally greet everyone with jumping up and kissing. If this is not acceptable behavior, you can correct him gently by telling him "No, off!" and pushing him away.

Enforce all rules now. If Rusty is not allowed to get up on the furniture, do not allow him to walk over your new couch. If he is not allowed in certain rooms, gate those rooms or keep the doors closed.

Beginning Housetraining

If Rusty starts sniffing and circling, immediately put him outside to relieve himself. Some Wheatens may become so excited that they forget to relieve themselves, but be patient and wait. Praise him when he urinates or defecates. If he starts to urinate or defecate inside the house, rush him outside and praise him when he relieves himself outside. Your surprise may be enough to correct it, but you may want to add "No!" when you catch your Wheaten relieving himself inside. Clear up the mess immediately with a pet odor enzymatic cleaner or a vinegar and water solution.

Crying

Your Wheaten may cry the first few nights. If you keep him in his crate by your bed, you can rap the crate and say "No, quiet!" Eventually, he will lie quietly.
- If you decide to try the TIP on this page, fill the hot water bottle with hot water and wrap it in a thick towel or blanket to prevent burning your puppy. Leave it aside for a short time, and then put your hand on it. If it is very warm or hot to the touch, use cooler water.
- Put the wrapped bottle in the puppy's crate.
- Put the alarm clock, with the alarm shut off, on top of your puppy's crate.
- Before returning home with your puppy, ask the breeder for a washcloth or rag that has the mother's scent on it, and put that in with your puppy.

All these things might help calm your puppy during the first few nights in his new home, but never leave the puppy alone with these items; he might chew them.

Note: You may be able to substitute a heating pad for the hot water bottle; however, you should keep it at the lowest setting and keep the elements and cord well hidden from puppy teeth. Some pet manufacturers make chew-proof heating mats. Remember, you should never leave a puppy or dog alone with an electrical device.

Crate-Training

There are two camps when it comes to crate-training: those who love it and those who have not had a dog who has yet destroyed their house. Those who do not use crates think crates are cruel, but check out the sidebar on the next page. When used properly, a crate will make training go much easier.

Crates are made either from plastic (airline travel crates) or wire, and should be just big enough for your Wheaten to stand up, turn around, and lie down. Crates are used as a training tool for housetraining (housebreaking) and for keeping your Wheaten out of mischief.

In most cases, you may want to get a crate that will fit a full-sized Wheaten and, if your Wheaten is a puppy, block off part of the excess crate so that he will not use the other side to relieve himself. (Some people use a box to fill the gap, or fashion a barrier from wire or wood.)

Getting your Wheaten used to a crate may take some time, so it is important to be patient with him. Put his bed in the crate and feed him in the crate. Leave the crate open so you can call him over and give him treats in the crate. The crate should be a place where only good things happen.

Start getting your Wheaten used to the crate by doing the following:

1. Put your Wheaten's food bowl with his breakfast or dinner in the crate and let him in to eat it. (Put the bowl in the back, so he must walk in all the way to eat.)

2. While he is eating, gently close the crate door. Before he is finished, open the crate door so he can walk out.

3. Do this with each meal and with any treats and toys he gets.

4. If he fusses, wait for him to settle down or give him another treat before opening the door. You do not want him to associate crying with being let out.

5. With each success, gradually lengthen the amount of time your Wheaten stays in the crate. You may have to give him treats every once in a while to enforce that this is a positive experience.

Aren't Crates Cruel?

Are crates cruel? In most cases, no. Crates simulate a wild canid's den. A crate, will give your puppy a spot where he can feel safe and cozy. It is a place that he can call his own and a place where he will feel secure. He will think of it as a den, even though it may be a funny-looking one to us humans.

Many people, when they look at a crate, think "cage," but they are anthropomorphizing the dog's feelings. Dogs do not consider crates as cages any more than they would consider a den or a hidey-hole as a cage.

Crates can, however, be abused. Never leave a puppy in a crate for longer than four hours at a time, and never leave an adult in a crate for longer than eight hours.

Eventually, you'll be able to increase the time your Wheaten spends in the crate. Use music such as light jazz or canine lullabies to signal a time when you wish your Wheaten to spend quiet crate time. Give him a puzzle toy filled with treats that he has to work at to get. He'll quickly associate crates with good things.

Use the crate for whenever you cannot watch your Wheaten. This includes when you go out, when you are busy, and when it is time for bed. Your Wheaten will appreciate the safe environment and a great toy to play with while you are gone.

HOW-TO: HOUSE-TRAINING

House-training or "house-breaking" as it is commonly called, is basically teaching your Wheaten to eliminate outside instead of inside. When you are first house-training your Wheaten, you should stick to a schedule. This schedule is very important because your Wheaten will rely on it until he is house-trained. Even then, he will expect to go out to eliminate during these times:

• When he first wakes up.
• Anytime after he eats or drinks.
• Before you go to school or work.
• Midday, around lunchtime.

• When you come home from school or work.
• After he plays or exercises vigorously.
• Before bedtime.

That may sound like a lot, but remember, small puppies and dogs who are not house-trained may not have the bladder control (or capacity) necessary to "hold it" very long. By putting your Wheaten on a schedule, he learns that he can expect to eliminate during certain times and thus waits for it.

Be aware that house-training can go very slowly or very quickly, depending on the dog, his age, and other factors.

For Puppies

House-training puppies can be a bit frustrating at first. For one thing, you might think that your puppy has figured it out one day, and the next day it seems he's forgotten everything. With some puppies, it can take six months to a year for them to be truly reliable.

• When your puppy first wakes up or after he eats, drinks, or plays, or when you come home or before you go to bed whisk him outside and put him in the area in which you wish him to eliminate. Give him a chance to eliminate—most puppies will use this time to investigate and play—and be patient!

• When your puppy eliminates outside, praise him! If he does not, you may have to play with him a bit or run around the yard with him. He will eventually squat and eliminate. Praise him.

• If your puppy was paper-trained, putting a small piece of newspaper out where you want him to go may entice him to eliminate.

• Another method to get your puppy to eliminate outside is to put his feces in the area you would like him to go, or you may try putting

down house-training pads sold in some stores. When he eliminates, again, praise him.
• Only have your puppy loose in your home when you can watch him. Otherwise, he needs to be crated.
• It can take a long time for a puppy to become reliably house-trained. Expect relapses for up to one year.
• Never make a puppy younger than six months "hold it" for more than four hours, with the exception of overnight. Even so, if he whines at night, you will need to let him out.
• Follow the training plan as outlined in the above section.

Be very patient with your puppy. Most puppies really are not house-trained for several months, even with you being vigilant.

For Older Dogs

House-training an older dog is usually a bit easier and generally takes less time than it does to house-train a puppy. But, you will need to first crate-train him, just as you would a puppy. Keep these things in mind:
• When your adult Wheaten first wakes up or after he eats, drinks, or plays, or when you come home or before you go to bed whisk him outside and put him in the area in which you wish him to eliminate. Give him a chance to eliminate—be patient!
• When your adult eliminates outside, praise him!
• Only have your dog loose in your home when you can watch him. Otherwise, he needs to be crated.
• Never make an adult "hold it" for more than nine hours.
• Follow the training plan as outlined in the above section.

• Lapses in your dog's house-training may signal health problems. Take him to the veterinarian to get checked out.

Accidents

What should you do if your Wheaten has an accident inside the house? While you may be tempted to "rub his nose in it" or swat him on the butt with a rolled-up newspaper, that is not very effective (and, in fact, most trainers think this is cruel). Instead, you need to be vigilant and watch for signs that your Wheaten is getting ready to eliminate. Sniffing around and squatting are definite signs, as is circling. If you catch him in mid-elimination, rush him outside to finish his business.

Now on to cleaning up the mess. Most cleaners are ammonia-based, and though to you they may give off a piney-fresh scent, it will not fool your Wheaten. In fact, these "cleaners" actually enhance the urine smell since urine is also ammonia-based. And if you do not completely get the urine or feces out, it will just tempt your Wheaten to eliminate there again. So, what do you do?

There are basically two methods for cleaning up accidents. One is to use a prepared enzymatic cleaner to clean up accidents, such as Nature's Miracle® (there are similar brands, so look at the label). Clean up what you can with paper towels and then follow up with the enzymatic solution (follow the directions on the label). The other method is to use soap and water to clean the mess and then follow it up with a white vinegar and water solution. The vinegar will counteract the smell.

BASIC OBEDIENCE

Although dog training is not rocket science, it does take a fair amount of timing and nuance, not to mention knowledge. Dogs, like humans, are not push-button creatures, and not all training methods work for all dogs although many do.

You have your wonderful Wheaten home! Not so wonderful, you say? He is chewing and destroying things in the house? He will not come when you call him? He jumps up on people?

Every dog needs basic obedience, and your Wheaten is no exception. In this chapter, we cover the basics of obedience training for a happier household.

Do-It-Yourself or Hire a Pro?

You know that you need to start training your Wheaten, but should you do it yourself or should you hire a professional trainer? Most people think nothing about hiring a plumber to install a new sink or about paying for an airline ticket instead of driving themselves someplace, so it is a little puzzling that people think that they should be experts when it comes to training a dog.

Although dog training is not rocket science, it does take a fair amount of timing and nuance, not to mention knowledge. Dogs,

like humans, are not push-button creatures, and not all training methods work for all dogs—although many do. Unless you are experienced in dog training, you may want to hire a professional trainer to "show you the ropes." A professional dog trainer can prevent you from making mistakes that can cause problems later on. She can watch and pinpoint problem areas for you and your dog. Lastly, she can help you correct bad habits your dog may have learned.

The cost of professional dog training can be nearly free or very inexpensive to several hundred dollars, depending on your location and where you go. Some shelters and pet supply stores offer low cost, basic obedience classes that work for most pets and pet owners but may not address serious issues such as aggression. In many cases you may get what you pay for and not much else. However, if you simply need to learn the basics, there is no reason to not try them out.

Let's say you want to train your dog by yourself. If you truly cannot afford to go the professional route, or you live in an area that

does not have many pet trainers, then by all means, go ahead and train your dog yourself. You can always look for a professional trainer if it does not work out.

Finding a Professional Trainer

So, how do you find a professional dog trainer? The first step is to look for a trainer who trains in mostly positive methods, such as positive-reinforcement and clicker training. The reasons for this are many, but basically you want a method that is gentle on your Wheaten. Wheatens are naturally sensitive dogs, being people dogs, so using a method that is kind and gentle is a good idea.

How do you go about finding a trainer? One way is to contact the Association of Pet Dog Trainers (www.APDT.com) and look for a referral in your area. While not all APDT trainers may suit your needs, it is a good place to start when looking for a trainer.

Another way to find a trainer is to ask your veterinarian, pet-owning friends, or even your

Wheaten's groomer. Most pet professionals know who is good out there and can give a good referral.

Once you have a referral, contact the trainer for an interview. Here are some questions you may wish to ask:

✔ How long have you been training dogs?
✔ Do you have any certifications?
✔ Do your dogs have any obedience or other titles?
✔ What types of training do you do? (beginners, competition obedience, agility)
✔ Do you use positive reinforcement? What types of training methods do you use?
✔ Do you train any Wheatens?
✔ How long are your classes?
✔ What days are your classes?
✔ How much do your charge?
✔ Can I sit in and watch a class?
✔ How large are your training classes?
✔ How are you at handling behavioral issues?
✔ Do you help me learn to train my dog?

✔ Do you have a guarantee?

✔ How old does my Wheaten need to be before he can attend class?

✔ What vaccinations will my pet need before entering class?

✔ What class would you recommend I and my Wheaten take?

✔ When is your next open class?

These questions are important because they will give you an idea how the trainer trains and whether this is the right trainer for you. All trainers should allow you to come in and watch a training class. If the trainer does not want you to watch because you might "steal his secrets," it is time to look elsewhere for a trainer.

When watching the trainer, look at how he or she handles the dogs. The trainer should be gentle and use only positive techniques. No jerking, hitting, slapping, or yelling. If the trainer uses harsh techniques, this is not the trainer for your Wheaten. The trainer should also be good at demonstrating and explaining concepts to owners. Does the trainer make the owners feel positive or does he or she belittle them? Is the trainer effective in his or her techniques?

After the class, you should be feeling positively about the trainer. If you have some reservations, you should probably consider other trainers before making a decision. After all, you need to feel good about working with this trainer; otherwise, you are unlikely to follow his or her instructions.

Once you find a trainer, enroll in the class and be sure to attend all of them.

Basic House Manners

Some people's pets. You know the type—they are always jumping on people, barking, and being general pests. Not your Wheaten? Really? Or is it?

When it comes to house manners, it is really up to you to determine what is acceptable and what is not. Unless your Wheaten is aggressive and a danger to people, your Wheaten's behavior is largely your choice. If you are fine with your Wheaten lying on the furniture, great! If you do not have a problem with your Wheaten jumping up on you to greet you, that is fine, too. Just be aware that certain behaviors have a tendency to snowball into something else. For example, it may be okay that your Wheaten lies on your old, worn couch, but what if you replace it with a new, expensive one? Your Wheaten is not likely to know the difference. Likewise, it may be fine for your Wheaten to jump on you, but not on Aunt Emma. Your Wheaten may not see much of a difference.

The truth is that as long as you are happy with your Wheaten's behavior, it does not really matter what his behavior is. The problem happens when his behavior is intolerable to others. So, before you let your Wheaten do something you think is cute, be sure to think through the possibilities.

Establish your house rules now and enforce them. Possible rules include:

✔ No chewing on inappropriate items.
✔ No urinating/defecating in the house.
✔ No excessive barking.
✔ No growling.
✔ No mouthing or biting.
✔ No jumping up on people.
✔ No climbing up on furniture.
✔ No begging at the table.
✔ No climbing on people.
✔ No humping people.
✔ No entering certain places in your house.

Many of these rules you will want to enforce. Others will be guidelines rather than actual rules.

Problem Wheatens

Wheatens are seldom difficult dogs. Wheatens become problematic when their owners let a particular situation get out of hand. In most cases, Wheatens are easygoing, but poorly trained or poorly bred dogs can be noisy, snappish, or even aggressive. They can be destructive, too.

Digging

Most Wheatens dig because they are terriers and dig out of boredom. If you leave your Wheaten outside all day, he is going to come up with something to amuse himself, and it just may happen to be digging.

Do not leave your Wheaten outside all day to the point where he is bored. Bring him inside, and if he is destructive inside, keep him in a crate with a puzzle toy or bone stuffed with yummy snacks. If he is digging while you are home and can watch him, you can put five to ten pennies in several soda pop cans, and when he is digging, shake the cans and toss them toward the hole (do *not* hit your Wheaten with them!). When he stops, praise him and give him something else to keep him occupied, like a toy.

Destructive Chewing

Most dogs love to chew, and Wheatens are no exception. The chew items can be rawhide chews, puzzle toys, assorted toys, and "indestructible" nylon bones, or they can be table legs, your IRS return, your new $200 pair of shoes, or a leather sofa. Anything is fair game when you leave a dog alone in your house—whether or not you intended it, you have just told Rusty, "Here are your toys—play!"

The easy solution is to keep your Wheaten crated when you leave the house or when you cannot watch him. While you are home, if he chooses something inappropriate, offer to "trade" something appropriate and possibly far tastier. For example, let's say Rusty has your leather shoes. Offer him a small rolled rawhide stick or a treat, and when he takes it, take the shoes away. Then, substitute an appropriate chew item: a marrowbone filled with peanut butter or chew toy.

Sometimes destructive chewing is associated with separation anxiety. See "Barking" on page 50 for more on separation anxiety.

Running Away

Although Wheatens are very much "people dogs," it is a good idea to never allow your Wheaten to run loose. Even if your Wheaten is trained for off-leash walks, all it takes is your dog finding something interesting to chase after and disaster can strike. But what about the escape artist or the dog that bolts through the door the moment you open it?

Thankfully, most Wheatens are not escape artists; however, there are always a few Houdini dogs in the group. Most owners of Houdini dogs put up inadequate barriers, and their dogs quickly get around the barriers

and receive the instant gratification of freedom. Rather than stopping the problem in its tracks, the owners continue to put up poorly thought-out barriers, and the dogs continue to escape. The escaping becomes a real problem as the owner puts up increasingly complex barriers only to have the dog get around them. Houdini dogs have been known to dig through concrete and bend steel-barred wolf cages!

Do not let the problem escalate to this point! If your Wheaten shows an inclination for escaping, put up fencing that is dig proof, climb proof, and jump proof. Also, do not

leave your Wheaten outside and unattended for hours with nothing to do. Your dog will use that time to analyze weaknesses in the defense and escape. Marrowbones or indestructible toys filled with peanut butter or other interesting snacks will provide hours of enjoyment.

Most escape artists are simply bored. Alleviate the boredom with regular activities. Soon escaping becomes less of a problem.

Dogs that bolt through doors are similar to the Houdini dog. Stop the behavior by teaching your Wheaten a new trick. When the doorbell sounds, either put him in his crate with a treat (move the crate closer to the door or purchase a separate one, if necessary) or put him into a *sit-stay* to wait for the treat. Once the door closes again, release your Wheaten and give him the treat.

Barking

Excessive barking and howling can be a result of boredom as well. Often, the dog sees something that catches his attention and barks. If he sees a reaction, such as a person jumping in surprise, his behavior is rewarded and he is more likely to bark again. He quickly turns into a nuisance barker who will bark at anything.

Do not leave your Wheaten outside alone during the day or while you sleep at night. Surprisingly, many owners of nuisance barkers are heavy sleepers and rarely hear their own dogs. If your dog barks while you are home, you may want to try the pennies-in-the-soda-pop-can method as mentioned in the digging section. When your Wheaten starts barking, toss a can so that it falls *near* him. (Do not hit your dog with the can!) Tell him "No! Quiet!" The noise should be enough to startle him.

There are bark collars and other anti-bark devices available. Some work by producing a loud, unpleasant, and distracting noise—these do not always work, especially if you have a dog that enjoys barking. Others work with electric shock, providing a very unpleasant stimulus. Do not use these collars because such shocks can cause a lot of pain on a dog the size of a Wheaten. There is a collar that sprays a mist of citronella under the dog's chin. Dogs do not like the spray and cease barking. Of all the bark collars, the citronella collar is probably the most humane and effective.

Nipping

Wheatens that nip or mouth are not cute. Never tolerate teeth on your skin for any reason. It is natural for any puppy to explore his new surroundings. Like babies, puppies are eager to pick things up. Because puppies do not have hands, they use their mouths to explore. Although this may be cute and harmless as a puppy, an adult dog who mouths is dangerous. Even a nip can break the skin. This is a serious problem that can turn into biting when your Wheaten is an adult.

If your Wheaten is a puppy, you can correct mouthing easily. When your Wheaten begins to mouth you, make a sudden, loud, startled noise, like "Ouch!" This will often scare him, and he will most likely stop and pull back. If he insists on chewing on you, hold your puppy's lower jaw in your fingers without hurting him and tell him firmly "No bite!" The puppy will usually whine because holding the lower jaw will make him uncomfortable. Let go of the jaw. If the puppy does not attempt to mouth

you, give him a treat or toy as a substitution. Say, "Good dog!" when he accepts the substitute. If he continues to mouth, repeat the above procedures. Usually a few times is all it takes for him to get the idea.

If your Wheaten is an adult and mouths, you can try the same techniques, but realize that an adult may behave very differently than a puppy. An adult that mouths, grabs clothing, or bites at hands and feet is a serious situation. You should consult a professional trainer.

Dominance and Aggression

Wheatens seldom have dominance problems, but it can happen. Dominance problems arise when you as the owner are unable to control your Wheaten. Dominance issues may be displayed through aggression, such as a growl or a snarl when you try to move your Wheaten off the couch to sit or when you touch him while he is eating his food. Other signs of dominance include leg humping, urinating on your bed or other furniture, and other negative behavior. Should your Wheaten behave in this fashion, first contact your veterinarian to be certain the problem is not biological. Some dogs with hidden injuries or conditions may snap when you try to pet them because they are experiencing pain. If the problem is not medical, you should then contact a dog behavior specialist—one that has experience with dominance problems.

Many dominance problems clear up when the owner and dog begin formal obedience training. This training focuses the dog on the owner and makes the owner the alpha in the dog's eyes.

There are five basic commands every Wheaten should know: *heel*, *sit*, *down*, *come*, and *stay*. Your Wheaten will be a more enjoyable companion if he is properly trained. There are many methods for teaching him these commands. The following methods use much positive reinforcement. Always have treats in your pocket ready to hand out when your Wheaten performs correctly.

Sit

Teaching Rusty to sit is relatively easy. Have Rusty standing beside your left side with a training collar

and leash on. With one hand, hold a treat over his nose, just out of reach and move it backward. With the other hand, lightly push down on his rump and say, "Rusty, sit!" Give Rusty the treat when his rump touches the floor. Practice *sit* often and always reward when Rusty performs correctly.

Down

Down tends to be a little more difficult to learn than *sit*. Have Rusty stand beside your left side with a training collar and leash on and tell him to *sit*. Hold a treat in the air, level with his nose. With a swift movement, bring the treat to the ground closer to Rusty's chest and say, "Rusty, down!" Rusty will hopefully try to follow the treat and drop to the ground. If he needs help to complete the *down*, you may lightly push on his shoulders. Give him the treat only when he is in the proper *down* position.

Never use the word "down" when you mean "off." Otherwise, Rusty may get confused when you tell him "Down!" He may jump off because you have been telling him "Down!" when you meant, "Get off the couch!"

Heel

Have Rusty sitting beside you on the left side with a training collar and leash on. Have a treat in your left hand. Say, "Rusty, heel!" and start walking, left foot forward. If Rusty starts to forge ahead or lag behind, get Rusty's attention by showing him the dog treat and lure him into the correct position. When he is in the correct position, praise him and give him a treat. If he lags because he is unsure, pat your leg and encourage him to come beside you. Likewise, if he forges ahead, gently pull him back using the leash or have him focus on the treat and lure him back. Give him the treat when he is in the proper position.

When you stop, have Rusty sit on your left side and give him a treat. When you start again, always start with the left foot forward. Dogs see the left leg movement before the right leg moves. Also, it becomes another signal to your Wheaten that he is to move with you.

Stay

Put Rusty on a leash on your left side and put him in a *sit* or *down* position. Tell him, "Rusty, stay!" and move your outstretched palm in a sweeping motion toward his face. Take one or two steps, right foot first this time, and turn around. If Rusty tries to follow you, say, "No, Rusty, stay!" and move Rusty back into his original position.

Rusty will eventually stay for a second or two. Before he stands up, give him a treat and quietly praise him, "Rusty, good stay!" If he stands, put him back in his place. Wait a few seconds and if he stays, give him a treat again. Give him another treat before releasing him. Release him after he stays for ten seconds. Continue working with him staying for only ten seconds a few feet away until he has mastered it. Give Rusty treats while he is maintaining his *stay*. You will eventually increase distance and time, but do not increase both simultaneously.

You may be able to guess when Rusty will break the *stay*. Try to give him a treat before it happens. Anytime Rusty shows nervousness or breaks his *stays* frequently, drop down to a shorter distance and a shorter time so he can have a successful *stay*. Remember: You always want to set your Wheaten up to succeed.

Release Rusty from his *stay* with the word "Okay." Walk over and praise your Wheaten for doing such a wonderful job.

Come

Start training for the *come* command by hooking a six-foot leather leash to Rusty's collar. Sit Rusty in *heel* position, give him the *stay* command, and go out to the end of the leash. Remember to leave with the right foot! This is an added signal that lets Rusty know he is to stay. Say, "Rusty, come!" and give a little tug on the leash. Your voice should be upbeat and happy. If Rusty does not come, reel him in

with gentle encouragement. Clap your hands and repeat the command if you have to make Rusty come more willingly. Give him a treat the moment he arrives and make a fuss over him.

Once Rusty recalls reliably on a six-foot leash, you can start lengthening the distance. You can accomplish this by using a long line, tracking lead, or a long retractable leash such as a Flexi-lead™. Practice your recalls in areas such as parks that have distractions. If Rusty can reliably come when called, you are both ready for the next step.

Put a light long line on Rusty with his leash so that when you take off the regular leash, you still have control, but Rusty is convinced he is off-leash. When you do so, practice in a secure area, such as an indoor training facility or a fenced-in backyard. Start from only ten feet away. Gradually lengthen the distance. Once Rusty proves he is reliable in a secure area, move to an unsecured area with many distractions. If you ever have to use the long line, go back to the leash and work on his on-leash recalls.

WHEATEN HEALTH

Although you can rely on your veterinarian to do most medical procedures, there are still some things you must do as a pet owner. Occasionally, you will need to give medicines to your dog and take your dog's temperature. In most cases, these procedures are easily accomplished.

One of the responsibilities of being a Wheaten owner is making certain that your Wheaten is healthy and free from diseases and parasites. Most basic health care you can do at home, but some requires a veterinarian. In this chapter, we cover caring for your Wheaten's health and choosing a veterinarian.

Choosing a Veterinarian

Choosing the right veterinarian is important for your Wheaten's health. If you do not like your dog's veterinarian, you are unlikely to trust the veterinarian's judgment, which could seriously compromise your dog's health. That is why it is important to find the right veterinarian for your Wheaten.

But how do you find the right veterinarian? The solution is as easy as asking some of your dog-owning friends who they would recommend. In many cases, they will be willing to give glowing recommendations for their own veterinarians. However, if your friends do not have any recommendations, you may have

to contact dog trainers or groomers in the area and ask who they take their dogs to and whether they would recommend a veterinarian. Often trainers and other dog professionals will readily recommend a veterinarian. If you still do not know, ask your dog's breeder if he or she has any recommendations for vets in your area. If not, perhaps they might know breeders in your area who would be willing to make a recommendation.

If you are still without a recommendation, you may have to search the Internet and look at veterinarians in your area. Though you may not have glowing recommendations for these veterinarians, you will at least have a place to start.

Once you have a list of veterinarians, you can now call them and ask questions to determine if any are right for you. (In most cases, you will be talking to the staff or vet techs who can answer your basic questions.) Many veterinarians offer other services such as boarding, grooming, and emergency care, so think about the kind of services you may need.

Here are some questions to ask:
- What are your hours?
- Do you offer after-hours or emergency on-call services?
- How long has the veterinarian been practicing veterinary medicine?
- Do you accept pet health insurance?
- Do you do payment plans or have financing available?
- How many veterinarians work at this practice?
- Do you offer boarding?
- Do you offer grooming?
- Do you have a mobile clinic or make house calls?
- Are you associated with a veterinary hospital or school?
- Do you have any specialists? What are your specialists?
- Does your veterinarian offer holistic services?
- Does your veterinarian see many Wheatens?
- Do you offer discount plans for multiple dogs?
- Do you sell specialty dog foods or prescription dog foods?

Not all these questions will be important to you, but many will be. For example, it is important to know that if your Wheaten gets sick, your veterinarian may be the one taking care of him, rather than a veterinarian who has never seen your dog before.

Once you have your answers, you have a decision to make depending on what is most important for you. You may decide that the veterinarian who has a groomer and has convenient hours is more important to you than a veterinarian who offers chiropractic for dogs and who offers boarding. Even so, you should keep that veterinarian in mind if your options are limited. Your next step is to visit the veterinarian and see the facilities.

Choose the veterinarian and vet clinic that most fits what you are looking for. Do not drop by unannounced, unless the veterinarian or veterinary staff says it is fine to do so. Most veterinary clinics are very busy Mondays, Fridays, and Saturdays, but may be very busy other times as well, so be sure to make an appointment. When you come by for a visit, look around. The facility should be clean and in proper repair. (If it has been a busy day, it might be in more disarray than usual.) There should be a waiting room with a large enough area for clients and their pets. In many facilities, it is common for the dog- and cat-waiting areas to be separated.

Watch the vet techs, front-desk staff, and veterinarian's work. Watch how they treat their clients and their pets. Are the animals treated kindly and gently? Or are they rushed through? Is it chaotic or is there a natural rhythm to things? Any veterinary clinic or veterinarian that gives you a bad feeling should be marked off your list. Remember, you must like the veterinarian, so even if he is well recommended, if you do not like him, go to your next choice.

If the clinic seems fine, your next step is to make an appointment for your Wheaten (for a checkup, vaccinations, or anything else your dog may need). If everything goes well, you now have found your new vet. If not, continue down the list of possible choices.

Listen to your veterinarian's recommendations as to caring for your pet's health. Ask questions. A good veterinarian will answer questions and will not make you feel foolish. Any veterinarian who makes you uncomfortable or who is unwilling to answer your questions to your satisfaction needs to be reconsidered.

Wheaten Hereditary Diseases

Renal Dysplasia (RD)

Renal dysplasia (or juvenile renal dysplasia) is a genetic disease in Wheatens that affects the kidneys; the kidneys are malformed and unable to function properly. Clinical signs of RD usually appear in affected Wheatens between the ages of four months and three years. Symptoms include excessive thirst and urination and can also include vomiting, weight loss, and sometimes diarrhea.

Breeders should test their puppies for RD as early as eight weeks of age with an ultrasound and a urine test. A renal biopsy may be more accurate, but it it is more invasive. If your breeder did not test your Wheaten for RD, you may want to have your veterinarian perform an ultrasound and a urine test to determine if the dog has this problem. The prognosis is not good for a long life, but your veterinarian can recommend a special low-protein diet and a course of treatment to help control it the best they can.

Protein-Losing Enteropathy (PLE) and Protein-Losing Nephropathy (PLN)

PLE/PLN is a condition in which either the intestines or the kidneys are unable to process protein correctly and actually lose protein. Unlike RD, PLE/PLN can occur anytime during the Wheaten's life and cannot be reliably screened for until the clinical signs are present. PLE/PLN is a genetic disease, but the mode of inheritance is unknown. Dogs with PLE or PLN will lose weight, show food allergies, and have diarrhea and vomiting. Veterinarians can diagnose PLE or PLN with a blood chemistry and urine test.

If there is a relationship between RD and PLE/PLN, it is currently unknown. More Wheatens have PLE/PLN than RD, and PLE/PLN may suddenly appear in lines that breeders thought to be free from it. Breeders try to screen for the disease, but it may appear in middle-aged or older dogs that have already been bred several times and produced puppies; therefore, a perfectly normal puppy from a reputable breeder may have PLE or PLN.

If your veterinarian diagnoses your Wheaten as having either PLE or PLN, he or she may prescribe a hypoallergenic diet that is wheat-free and has a novel protein source (see "Food Allergies," just below, for more information).

Food Allergies

Ironically, a common food allergy in the Wheaten Terrier is wheat or wheat gluten. Wheatens may also show allergies to corn, chicken, lamb, and milk products. These allergies may be a result of PLE or PLN or another genetic factor. Wheatens exhibiting food allergies may have itchy skin and dermatitis or may have gastric upset, weight loss, vomiting, and diarrhea. If Rusty shows any of these symptoms, have him tested for PLE/PLN.

Some dogs have shown allergies to lamb and rice diets. At one time, veterinarians and nutritionists considered lamb hypoallergenic because it was relatively unavailable as a dog food source. As lamb and rice diets have become popular, increasing numbers of dogs have become allergic to lamb. Your veterinarian can prescribe a diet with a novel protein source.

Anesthesia Sensitivity

Wheatens may exhibit sensitivity to anesthetics similar to sight hounds and northern breeds. Due to this sensitivity, you should make sure your veterinarian takes precautions.

The Health Check

You can take an active role in your Wheaten's health by performing a health check on him at least once a week. You can do a full health check anytime you have a few minutes to spend with your Wheaten. Many owners like to perform the health check while they are grooming their dogs.

The health check provides several benefits:
- It familiarizes you with your Wheaten's anatomy; what is normal and what is not.
- It provides extra social time that you might not normally spend with your Wheaten.
- It will alert you to potential health problems before they become serious.
- It will teach your Wheaten to accept handling even in tender or ticklish areas.

Go slowly and gently the first few times you perform a health check, especially if your Wheaten is not used to being handled quite so much. It does not really matter at which end you start the health check as long as your Wheaten is comfortable with it. Follow these steps when doing the health check:

1. When beginning the health check, be sure to perform it the same way each time, so that it becomes a routine. That way, you are sure not to skip over anything.

2. If you find something that looks or feels strange, try looking for it on the opposite side. Normal features are usually symmetrical, but if you are not sure what is normal, ask your veterinarian.

3. If you find something abnormal, it is time to schedule a visit with the veterinarian. Only your veterinarian can determine the proper treatment.

For the sake of simplicity, this list starts at the head and goes to the tail. Remember, you can start wherever you would like, but be sure to do it the same way each time.

1. Head—Look for lumps and bumps that might indicate tumors. Look for rashes, red areas, and scaly skin.

2. Ears—Is there is a foul odor or a grainy, waxy substance in the ear? Is the ear reddened or inflamed? These could be signs of ear mites or an ear infection.

2. Eyes—Are the eyes clear and bright with no signs of redness? There should be no excessive discharge or weeping. There should be no pus or yellow or green discharge.

4. Nose—The nose should be moist and cool to the touch. There should not be a discharge. Your dog's nose should not be scaly or raw. Excessive sneezing also indicates a possible problem.

5. Mouth—The mouth should be sweet smelling and free of "doggy breath." The teeth should be clean and white and free from plaque and tartar. The gums should be pink and healthy, not red or inflamed. Look for broken teeth or teeth that have turned brown, indicating a possible tooth problem. Look inside for strange growths and bumps, as these can indicate oral tumors or abscesses. If your Wheaten is older than six months, look for puppy teeth that have not come out yet.

6. Skin and coat—Look (and feel) over your Wheaten's entire body for lumps and bumps. Sores, tender red spots, and lumps (especially those that are warm to the touch) are not

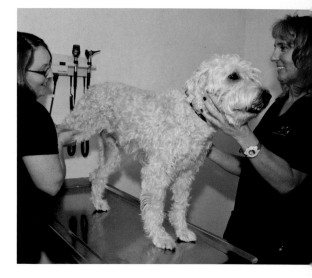

normal. Look for fleas and ticks as well. Grainy red, brown, or black pieces of dirt that turn red when wet are signs of flea infestation.

7. Legs and feet—Feel down your dog's legs for unusual lumps and bumps, watching for any signs of tenderness. When feeling a lump, check the other leg to see if it is symmetrical. Move the leg through its natural range of motion (do not force it into odd positions). The movement should be fluid and there should be no clicks or pops.

8. Examine your Wheaten's feet—Look at the top, at the bottom, and in between the toes. Check for broken nails. Look for redness, lumps, and sore or cut pads. Redness of the hairs around the feet indicates excessive licking and may indicate allergies.

9. Back and abdomen—Feel along your Wheaten's spine and ribs. (You should be able to feel his ribs without searching. If you cannot, your Wheaten may be obese.) Feel for lumps and bumps in these areas and look for fleas and flea droppings especially along the base of the tail and the abdomen. If your Wheaten is hunched up or shows tenderness around the lower back where the kidneys are, this may be a sign of a more serious condition.

10. Sexual organs and anus—If your Wheaten is female and spayed, there should be no discharge coming from her sexual organs. If she is intact, there should only be a light discharge during her estrus or heat (any other discharge is a serious problem). Males can have a small discharge but nothing that suggests an infection. The anus should not be irritated nor should there be growths around it. If you see something that looks like grains of rice near your dog's anus, he may have a case of tapeworm infestation.

Vaccinations

Follow your veterinarian's recommendations concerning vaccinations. In most cases, if you bought or adopted your Wheaten as a young puppy, your veterinarian will probably recommend two or three combination vaccinations three or four weeks apart and then a rabies vaccination sometime after four months. An adult Wheaten will need vaccinations once every year or every three years, depending on the type of vaccination and also your Wheaten's potential for exposure to dangerous diseases. For example, a Wheaten who is more or less a homebody is usually at less risk than a dog who is boarded or who travels.

Most Wheatens need to be vaccinated against distemper, parvovirus, canine adenovirus 1 and 2, infectious canine hepatitis and rabies, but this should be under the recommendation of your veterinarian. Other vaccinations for coronavirus, leptospirosis, bordetella, giardiasis and Lyme disease are optional and need to be given only if there is a particular risk of contracting the disease. For example, if you board your Wheaten, you will need to vaccinate him against bordetella, that is, kennel cough; or if you live in a Lyme disease–prone area where you walk with your Wheaten, you may wish to consider a Lyme vaccine for your Wheaten. Ask your veterinarian for his or her recommendations.

If you bought your Wheaten from a breeder, you should have also received the vaccination records for your puppy. If you do not have the vaccination records or cannot get them, you will have to have your veterinarian vaccinate your dog as soon as possible.

Vaccinations are very important, so do not skip them. They protect your dog against deadly diseases, such as parvovirus, rabies, and distemper. Young puppies and elderly dogs are more susceptible to diseases than adult dogs, but any dog can contract and die from these diseases.

Spaying and Neutering

Spaying is removing the uterus and ovaries from the female dog and neutering removes the testicles from the male dog. If you have been a pet owner for any length of time, you have probably heard that spaying and neutering is a good idea to prevent unwanted litters and a way to prevent pet overpopulation.

If you have bought from a reputable breeder or a shelter, they may have already had your puppy spayed or neutered before coming home.

But if you have not spayed or neutered your Wheaten yet, you may be wondering why you should. After all, you may think that you might recoup the cost of the dog by breeding her,

right? But the truth is, spaying or neutering is a healthy option for your Wheaten. With these procedures, you can actually help prevent or even eliminate certain health problems. Let's look at the benefits:

• It eliminates the heat cycle; you do not have to worry about the mess or about strange dogs visiting.
• It eliminates the urge to roam to look for mates.
• It helps curb aggression in both males and (arguably) females.
• It prevents unwanted pregnancies and makes you a responsible pet owner.
• It reduces or eliminates certain types of tumors and cancers in your dog. In males, it eliminates the chance of testicular cancer and greatly reduces anal tumors. In females, it eliminates the chance of ovarian and uterine cancers and greatly reduces breast cancer, if done before the dog's second estrus or heat.
• It virtually eliminates pyometra—a deadly condition affecting females.

Any competent vet can perform a spay or neuter. It requires anesthesia and an overnight stay at the vet clinic and then a quick visit to the vet clinic to remove the stitches ten to fourteen days later.

Internal Parasites

Question: Can I get pinworms from my Wheaten? The answer is no. Pinworms only infect humans and can only be contracted through contact with someone who has pinworms or by handling diapers of infants or toddlers who have them.

However, there are plenty of internal parasites that can make your Wheaten sick. These parasites can, in some cases, kill your Wheaten, or at least severely hurt his health, if they are not eliminated. Let's look at the most common ones:

Worms: Worms are a problem because they feed on either the nutrition that is meant for your Wheaten or they feed directly on your Wheaten's blood, thus threatening his life through anemia. Although you usually cannot get worms from direct contact with a dog who has worms, you can contract worms through the feces, or from dirt that has been contaminated with infected feces, of a dog who has the worms by accidentally ingesting the dirt or fecal matter (children who eat dirt and those who do not practice proper sanitation are most at risk). Here are some of the most common worms:

• Hookworms (*Ancylostoma caninum*) are worms that feed off of blood in the small intestine. Your Wheaten can contract them through penetration of the skin or through his mother before he was born or while nursing.

• Roundworms (*Toxocara canis*) are the most common worms that infest dogs. These worms can infest the intestines, stomach, and lungs (when migrating) and feed off the nutrition your dog needs. Your Wheaten can contract them through ingesting contaminated soil or feces, or through his mother before he was born or while nursing. You can occasionally see roundworms in stools or your dog may cough one up.

• Tapeworms (*Dipylidium caninum*) are worms that live in the intestines. These worms are usually contracted through fleas (the dog bites and swallows a flea), but occasionally a dog might contract them through eating raw game or rodents. Tapeworms often look like grains of rice around your dog's anus.

• Whipworms (*Trichuris vulpis*) are worms that feed off of blood in the intestine. Dogs contract whipworms by eating contaminated soil or feces.

Because worms are such a health threat, you should never ignore the signs of having worms, such as poor hair/coat, garlic breath, listlessness, pieces of worm around the anus or in the fecal matter, pot belly, diarrhea, vomiting, or eating without gaining weight. In many cases, there may not be any signs until your dog's health is severely affected.

Do not use over-the-counter dewormers as these may not treat the worms your Wheaten may have. Over-the-counter wormers can be dangerous if used incorrectly. Instead, bring a fecal sample to your veterinarian, and he will identify the type of worms and prescribe the appropriate treatment.

Heartworm: Heartworm is a deadly parasite your Wheaten can contract. Heartworm is prevalent through most of the continental United States, although it is rarer in the Rocky Mountain west.

Mosquitoes transmit heartworm after feeding on an infected dog. The mosquito picks up the microfilariae or heartworm larvae, and the larvae incubate in the mosquito for several days. The mosquito then goes and feeds off another dog, injecting the microfilariae into another dog, thus infecting him. The heartworm larvae eventually move to the heart and lungs and even the veins in the liver. If left untreated, the dog will die from heartworm.

Treating heartworm is somewhat risky and very expensive. It is safer, more cost effective, and certainly healthier for your Wheaten to prevent heartworm in the first place with heartworm preventatives. The latest guideline suggests that dogs should stay on heartworm preventatives year-round and be tested yearly.

Basic Medical Skills Every Owner Needs

Although you can rely on your veterinarian to do most medical procedures, there are still some things you must do as a pet owner. Occasionally, you will need to give medicines to your dog and take your dog's temperature.

In most cases, these procedures are easily accomplished. However, some dogs are more difficult to work with. If you find you are having struggles with any of these procedures, ask your veterinarian for help.

Taking Your Wheaten's Temperature

There are now two ways you can take your dog's temperature. At one time, the only option was to use the rectal method. Nowadays, however, that has changed because there are ear thermometers that take your dog's temperature as fast as your doctor takes yours. However, these thermometers can be a bit pricey and many dogs' ears do not work well with them. So, you may find that you must take your dog's temperature rectally.

If this is the case, be sure to use an unbreakable electronic thermometer that can be used rectally. Wash the end thoroughly with soap and water, and then rinse it with isopropyl alcohol. Use petroleum jelly (Vaseline™) to lubricate it, then turn it on and wait until it is ready. While holding your dog quietly, gently insert the end into your dog's rectum. Insert it far enough so it will get a good reading, but do not force it in (about a half inch for a puppy and no more than an inch for an adult).

Wait until the thermometer beeps before removing it. Wipe the thermometer off with a paper towel and read it. Normal temperatures for dogs are from 100°F to 102.5°F.

Giving Your Dog a Pill

Occasionally, your veterinarian may require you to give your dog a pill. Some dogs are terrific with taking a pill, but many are not. So if yours is not good with pills, try the following:

1. Ask your veterinarian if the pill is in a chewable or otherwise tasty form. Sometimes, the veterinarian can have the pill compounded in a tasty flavor so the pill is easier for your dog to swallow.

2. If the pill is not in a chewable form, ask your vet if the pill can be given with food. If it can, try Pill Pockets brand treats. These treats are very tasty and have a pocket to slip the pill inside. Most dogs will unknowingly swallow dog's mouth and gently tilt his head back while stroking his throat until he swallows.

=== T I P ===

The Skin Snap Test

The skin snap test is a way for pet owners to determine if their dog is becoming dehydrated. Pull the skin up behind the dog's neck close to the shoulder blades. If the skin snaps back, the dog is hydrated. If it melts back, or worse, stays in position, the dog is severely dehydrated and needs veterinary attention.

Another way to test for hydration is to feel the inside of the dog's mouth. If it is sticky, he is dehydrated and needs fluids and most likely veterinary attention.

Dehydration is an emergency, so do not delay bringing your Wheaten to the vet if your Wheaten is dehydrated. This is a serious, life-threatening condition.

Do this test while your dog is healthy so that you know what is normal. Age and loose skin will determine how quickly the skin "melts" back.

the pill whole with the Pill Pockets because they enjoy the treat. Alternatives to this would be to hide the pill in cheese, peanut butter, or some meat.

3. If you cannot give your dog's pill with food or if your dog is clever enough to spit out the pill, you may have to purchase a piller or pill gun. This little device allows you to put the pill in one end. Slip that end into your Wheaten's mouth so that the pill is situated in the back of your dog's mouth and push the plunger. Remove the pill gun and close your

dog's mouth and gently tilt his head back while stroking his throat until he swallows.

Giving Your Dog Liquid Medicine

Sometimes, your dog's medicine comes in a liquid rather than a pill form. Like pilling, you have several methods available for giving medications.

1. Ask your vet if the medicine can be given with food. Squirting and mixing the medicine in some yummy canned food can make medicine time a yummy experience. (See if there are flavors such as liver or chicken that it can be compounded with.)

2. If the medicine is to be given without food, see if they have flavors that make it less odious to give.

3. If the medicine is to be given without food and the dog refuses to eat it directly or there are no flavors, ask your vet for an oral syringe. Fill the syringe to the mark, slip it into your dog's mouth, and squirt the medicine in. Remove the syringe, close your dog's mouth and gently tilt his head back while stroking his throat until he swallows.

Diarrhea and Vomiting

Diarrhea and vomiting are common dog ailments. In most cases, unless the diarrhea is severe (meaning it lasts more than a day and is not affected by over-the-counter antidiarrheal medicines, or is dark, tarry diarrhea, or is bloody or with mucus), giving an over-the-counter antidiarrheal medicine is all that is needed (ask your veterinarian for the proper dosages) or a kaolin product that is available through veterinary supply stores or on the Internet (be sure to follow the dosage instructions). Be sure your dog has access to water as diarrhea can dehydrate him quickly. Dehydration is an emergency, so do not wait to bring him to the veterinarian if he is becoming dehydrated. (See the TIP box on the skin snap test.) You can help rehydrate him by offering him unflavored Pedialyte.

When your dog has diarrhea, withhold food for the first twenty-four hours, and then after that, feed your Wheaten a mix of boiled hamburger and rice (assuming he is not allergic to either; otherwise consult your vet) for the next day. If his stomach can tolerate that, you can start mixing in his regular food again.

Vomiting once is not necessarily a cause for concern, but if your Wheaten projectile vomits, vomits frequently, starts becoming dehydrated, has blood or what looks like black coffee grounds in the vomit, or retches without vomiting, you must seek veterinary attention.

Should I Breed My Wheaten?

At some point, you may consider breeding your Wheaten. Maybe it is because you paid a fair amount of money for her or maybe you would like a puppy who is "just like" your current dog. But maybe you have heard about pet overpopulation and are not sure about whether or not you should breed your dog.

Misconceptions About Breeding Dogs

Oddly enough, people have a fair number of misconceptions when it comes to breeding dogs. First of all, a pet owner may think that this is a lucrative way to make money. In many cases, this simply does not happen. The cost of breeding a dog should start with health checks and health certifications (OFA and CERF as mentioned in Chapter 2). These can cost hundreds of dollars to do in order to prove that the dog is healthy and will produce healthy offspring. Then, consider the stud fee, the cost of prenatal care, and the cost of whelping and caring for the pups. That will include the cost of dewormings, vaccinations, and taking care of any health problems that may arise. And that is assuming that there are no complications with the pregnancy or whelping. By the end, a breeding could cost the owner thousands of dollars, not to mention the distinct possibility of losing the female.

Then, of course, there is the placement of the puppies. How do you know if the owners you sell them to will be as kind and loving as you? Will you be able to sell them for a price that will help you recoup the amount of money you have spent taking care of these puppies?

Do people make money breeding dogs? Sure they do. But in most cases, those are puppy mills in which the breeders do not really care much about the dogs or the puppies except as a profit margin.

Other myths about breeding dogs tend to go somewhere along the line that breeding a female will "improve her personality" or "settle her down." The truth is that breeding may change your dog's personality but not in the way you intended! Breeding does not improve a dog's health one bit. On the other hand, spaying will improve her health if you spay your dog young enough (see "Spaying and Neutering" earlier in this chapter).

But what if you want a puppy "just like" your current dog? The reality is that not even your dog's offspring will be "just like" your dog. Your dog is a unique individual, and you are not going to be able to replicate him or her by producing puppies. In fact, because your dog is a crossbred dog, chances are you will not breed a dog very much like your current dog. Wheatens do not "breed true" when bred to other Wheatens, so you may end up with a litter that looks nothing like your current Wheaten. So, enjoy your dog, and consider, instead, not adding to the many homeless dogs out there.

For more information on becoming a responsible breeder: If you still wish to become a breeder, you should do your research on the Wheaten and other dog breeds. Contact the Soft Coated Wheaten Terrier Club of America and talk with other Wheaten breeders. Read all you can about how to become a responsible breeder and learn what it takes to produce high-quality puppies. If you can, find a mentor who will help you. A good mentor will tell you both the good and bad about being a dog breeder.

The Older Wheaten

At some point, you may notice a little graying on your Wheaten's muzzle or perhaps he is a little stiff when he gets up in the morning. When did your Wheaten get old? Gone are the silly puppy days, and now you can relax with a friend who has been with you for many years.

Your Wheaten will need special care during this time as well.

How Long Will a Wheaten Live?

Most people wonder how long their dog may live. There are varying circumstances, such as hereditary factors, but there are also factors such as good nutrition and proper care that will help your Wheaten live as long as he can. A dog who is healthy and well cared for could live ten to fifteen years. Unfortunately, there are debilitating diseases such as cancer that can cut his life short. Even then, however, there are cancer survivors who live well past ten years of age with treatment.

Common Diseases: With old age come old-age diseases. Many of these diseases are treatable but not completely curable. Your job is to make sure your dog is comfortable and

happy. Here are some conditions your Wheaten may get as he ages:

• Arthritis—Includes stiffness and pain in the joints. Some supplements, such as glucosamine and MSM (found in Cosequin, Glycoflex, or Synova-Cre), can help relieve arthritis. These supplements work well on some dogs, yet do nothing for others. Your vet can help mitigate some of the effects of arthritis with anti-inflammatories. (Do not give your dog either acetaminophen or ibuprofen—they are very poisonous to dogs.)

• Blindness—That is, loss of sight in one or both eyes. You may not even notice if your dog goes blind. Most dogs are quite adept at getting around their home and even their neighborhood even though they are blind. The owner usually notices something is amiss when the dog bumps into something on the floor that perhaps normally is not kept there. Have your veterinarian confirm your suspicions if you think your dog is blind. Depending on the type of eye problem, veterinary advances have helped restore dogs' sight, so speak with your veterinarian about this.

• Cancer and Tumors—The possibility of cancer and tumors is more prevalent with age. If you find a lump or bump that is not normally on your dog, have it checked immediately. Some cancers and tumors are fast-spreading, and if you wait too long, it may be too late for your veterinarian to do anything about them. Signs of cancer include strange growths, excessive weight loss, lack of appetite, bleeding, sores or wounds that will not heal, abnormal swellings, excessive sleep or lethargy, and difficulty breathing, eating, or drinking.

• Cognitive Dysfunction Syndrome (CDS)—Cognitive Dysfunction Syndrome is similar to Alzheimer's disease in dogs. Your Wheaten may suddenly look "lost" in the room. He may not recognize loved ones and may forget his housetraining. His sleep may be disrupted, and he may bark and carry on in the middle of the night. Your veterinarian can diagnose and perhaps treat CDS.

• Deafness—If your Wheaten is not listening to you, perhaps he is deaf. Have your veterinarian examine him for deafness. There are hearing aids available for dogs.

• Dental problems—Stinky breath, bleeding gums, loss of appetite, broken teeth, or a buildup of brown tartar or plaque indicate the need to go to the vet for a teeth cleaning and possible extraction.

• Heart problems—Coughing, swelling of the legs, lethargy, and shortness of breath are all signs of an existing heart problem. Have your veterinarian check your Wheaten for problems.

Your vet may be able to treat the condition with a special diet and medications.

• Kidney/Bladder problems—Incontinence, excessive water drinking, blood in the urine, or dark- or light-colored urine may all be a sign of kidney or bladder problems. Your veterinarian can prescribe medications and perhaps a special diet to treat your Wheaten's condition.

In most cases, these problems require veterinary attention. Keep a careful watch over the changes in your dog—they may be subtle and gradual over time. Keep a diary on his condition so that you can refer back to how he looked and felt even a few weeks ago. If there is a marked change, take him to the veterinarian.

Caring for the elderly dog: Caring for an elderly dog requires a bit of foresight. He cannot run as fast or as far as he used to, and he may want to nap more by a warm fire than go outside exploring. As your dog ages, he will appreciate a warm house and a warm, soft bed. (There are orthopedic beds for dogs available.) He may have to relieve himself more often and may not be able to "hold it" like he could when he was young.

Older dogs have a harder time climbing up onto furniture or getting into a car, so consider getting a pet ramp (available at pet supply stores and on the Internet). Your dog will need a special diet for seniors, too, so talk with your veterinarian about what is recommended in terms of dog food.

Lastly, your senior dog may be losing his eyesight and hearing. This is not the time to rearrange the furniture. Do not get angry or frustrated at him because he is not listening to you. Chances are good that his hearing has faded, and he does not realize you are calling him.

Above all, be patient with your old friend.

Euthanasia: Saying good-bye is perhaps the hardest part of being a dog owner. Do not allow your best friend to suffer needlessly. If your dog is in great pain or the prognosis is not good, talk with someone who is clear-headed who can give you good advice. Though it is tempting to try heroic actions to save your pet, you may discover that the end result is still the same. Dogs do not live forever, and it may not be humane or in anyone's capability to save him.

Euthanasia is painless and quick. The veterinarian will administer an injection. Your pet will simply fall into a deep sleep and pass away comfortably. You can stay with your Wheaten during his final minutes or leave—it is your choice.

You will grieve. This is normal and natural. Talk to your vet about grief. He or she may be able to refer you to free or low-cost pet-loss counseling. Many veterinary colleges offer free or low-cost pet-loss hotlines.

With time, the pain and anguish of your pet's death will fade. You will start remembering all the good times you had together. Perhaps, in time, you will be ready to own another Wheaten again.

Emergencies

Emergencies happen, no matter how careful you are. Be sure you are prepared for an emergency with a first-aid kit and the emergency veterinarian's numbers handy.

Assembling a First-Aid Kit

Every household with a dog should have a first-aid kit. You can assemble one from easily purchasable items:

- Large and small nonstick bandage pads
- Sterile gauze wrappings
- Sterile sponges
- Pressure bandages
- Self-adhesive wrap (VetWrap™)

- Disposable latex gloves
- Triple antibiotic ointment or nitrofurizone (Nitrofurizone is available through veterinary supply catalogues.)
- Bandage tape
- Surgical glue or VetBond™ (available through veterinary supply catalogues)
- Cortisone cream
- Quick muzzle
- Rectal thermometer
- Unflavored pediatric electrolyte (Pedialyte™)
- Syrup of Ipecac™
- Betadine solution
- Bandage scissors
- Petroleum jelly (Vaseline™)
- Mineral oil
- Kaolin product (Kaopectate™)
- Aspirin
- Hydrogen peroxide
- Tweezers
- Your veterinarian's phone number, pager, after-hours number
- An emergency veterinary hospital's phone number
- Local poison control center's phone number

Muzzling Your Dog: In an emergency, you may have to muzzle your Wheaten. Even the gentlest dog may bite if frightened or injured. Have a quick muzzle (sold in pet supply stores and through mail order) available. If you do not have one, you can fashion a makeshift muzzle from rope, a belt, or tie. Note: Do not muzzle a dog that is having problems breathing!

Start in the middle at the bottom of the dog's muzzle. Wrap the bandage upward, tie, and then bring it back downward under the chin and tie. Take the two loose ends and tie them behind the dog's head securely.

How to Recognize an Emergency

In most cases, it is pretty easy to decide that your dog needs to go to the vet, but sometimes it is difficult to know whether or not you should. Here is a handy chart to help you determine if it is time to get your dog to an emergency vet:

- Dog is unconscious or unresponsive.
- Dog is not breathing.
- Dog is bleeding from a major gash, puncture wound, or other wound.
- Dog has a broken bone or bones.
- Dog is in distress, whimpering or crying.
- Dog is choking.
- Dog is retching, drooling, or pacing nervously.
- Dog's stomach is distended, or dog is trying to defecate or retches often.
- Dog's temperature is 103°F or above, or dog's temperature is 99°F or below.
- Dog has graying gums or mucus membranes.
- Dog is having seizures or convulsions.
- Dog is in obvious pain.
- Dog has a severe injury such as one to the eye, face, ears, or to any area of the body.

Emergency Treatments

The following is a short list of possible emergencies you may encounter. As with all emergencies, seek veterinary attention immediately and follow your veterinarian's instructions.

Dehydration: Dehydration can occur anytime and may show up as weakness, extreme thirst, and failure for the skin to snap back around the muzzle or neck. In extreme cases, you will see pale gums, and the dog may go into shock, and possibly die. Dehydration is often associated with heatstroke, but the

outside temperature does not need to be warm to have a dog experience dehydration. Vomiting, diarrhea, and physical exertion can all cause dehydration.

Treat the condition that caused the dehydration and offer an unflavored pediatric electrolyte solution or water and seek veterinary attention.

Prevent dehydration by always providing water from a known good source. In the winter, provide outdoor water in a heated bucket or bowl.

Heatstroke: Signs of heatstroke include dehydration, extreme thirst, watery diarrhea, vomiting, high temperature (over 103°F), difficulty breathing, lethargy, weakness, and pale gums.

Do not muzzle a dog with heatstroke or you will worsen the condition. Move him into a shady or air-conditioned area with good air circulation. Offer water or an unflavored pediatric solution to drink. Soak the dog in tepid or cool water. Note: Ice-cold water will cause capillaries to contract and not dissipate heat. Make certain the dog can breath by removing constricting collars or other items. Seek immediate veterinary attention.

Prevent heatstroke by keeping your dog in a cool, well-ventilated place with plenty of shade during the summer. Avoid exercising in extremely warm and humid weather. Always provide fresh water to avoid dehydration. Never leave your dog in a car in warm weather.

Choking and Difficulty Breathing: A dog that is choking or is having difficulty breathing will cough or gag. The gums or tongue will turn blue or pale. Do not muzzle the dog. Loosen all collars and any other items that may restrict breathing and seek immediate veterinary attention.

You may be able to see what your Wheaten is choking on. Do not try to reach in with your fingers to remove the object; you may accidentally push it farther down your dog's throat. Use tweezers to remove it, if it is small enough.

Otherwise, try pushing on your dog's abdomen to expel the object. If your dog stops breathing, administer mouth-to-mouth resuscitation.

Cuts, Injuries, and Deep Puncture Wounds: You can clean minor cuts and scrapes yourself with a 10-percent betadine/90-percent water solution. Then apply a triple antibiotic ointment and watch for signs of infection.

For serious injuries, such as deep cuts and injuries from car accidents, seek immediate veterinary attention. Deep cuts may require suturing. Stop the bleeding using pressure bandages, except in serious crushing injuries. If the injury is severe, such as being hit by a car, there may be internal bleeding, broken bones, and spinal injuries. Use a stiff board to transport the dog (carefully slide the board under the dog), and seek immediate veterinary attention.

For deep puncture wounds, first determine how deep the puncture is. If the object is still embedded, do not remove it if practical, and seek immediate veterinary treatment. If the puncture is a dog bite, and the bite is not serious, you can clean the wound with a betadine/water solution. Your veterinarian may wish to prescribe antibiotics to prevent infection. Be certain that both your dog and the biting dog have had their current rabies vaccinations.

Poisoning: In the event your dog has gotten into a poisonous substance, contact your veterinarian or local poison control center and have the substance or chemical available so you can properly describe the poison. Follow the veterinarian or poison control center's instructions. Do not induce vomiting unless told to do so. Some acids, alkalis, and other substances can cause even more harm for your dog if aspirated.

Electric Shock: In this situation, do not touch your dog or you may be electrocuted also. Use a wooden broom handle or other nonconductive item to unplug the cord. Treat this emergency the same as you would for shock by maintaining proper body temperature, and seek emergency veterinary treatment. Administer mouth-to-mouth resuscitation by closing the dog's mouth and breathing into his nose if the dog is not breathing.

Burns: A severe burn, where the skin is charred or underlying tissue is exposed,

═══ T I P ═══

Mouth-to-Mouth Resuscitation

If your dog has stopped breathing, perhaps the only way to save his life is to give mouth-to-mouth resuscitation. Start by removing the dog's collar and any other constricting device, and make certain your dog's airway is clear. Close his mouth, hold his jaws together, and blow gently into his nose. Do not blow hard or overinflate his lungs or you may rupture a lung. You should see his side move only as if he were breathing. Now release and let the air leave the lungs. Breathe into his nose again and release. Continue to do this until your dog is breathing on his own.

requires immediate veterinary attention. You can treat minor burns over a small area with ice packs or cold water. Do not use water on extensive burns or you may risk shock. Aloe vera is a good burn treatment after the burn has blistered.

Broken bones: Fractures to the head, chest, or back may be life threatening. Use a stiff board to transport the dog (carefully slide the board under the dog), and seek immediate veterinary attention. If your dog has broken his leg, you can fashion a splint from a stick, a rolled-up piece of stiff cardboard, or even a rolled-up newspaper. Put the splint alongside the broken leg and wrap either VetWrap™ or tape around it. Transport your dog to the veterinarian immediately.

NUTRITION

Nowadays, pet owners have many choices when it comes to their pet's nutrition. News stories about tainted food have made many pet owners switch to homemade diets, but professionals question whether pets are getting the nutrition they need. What should you do?

"Garbage in, garbage out," the old saying goes. What is true for computers is true when it comes to nutrition and dogs. Your Wheaten will live longer and will look and feel his best when he is fed a balanced diet with optimal nutrition. In this chapter, we talk about nutrition and what makes for a good diet for your Wheaten.

Do-It-Yourself or Store-Bought?

Should you buy a commercial dog food or make your own? Nowadays, pet owners have many choices when it comes to their pet's nutrition. News stories about tainted food have made many pet owners switch to homemade diets, but professionals question whether pets are getting the nutrition they need. What should you do?

Note: The dog on the opposite page was given a "pet trim" and, therefore, looks different from the other dogs pictured in this book.

At one end of the spectrum, there is the do-it-yourself dog food person. If you are convinced that commercial pet food is tainted, then this is the route you should take. (See "Homemade Diets" later in this chapter). On the other end is the person who implicitly trusts in commercial pet food and will buy whatever food the dog will eat. In most cases this is safe, with the exception of recalled dog foods.

Most pet owners fall somewhere in the middle. The pet food recall has shaken many pet owners' beliefs about commercial dog food, and the savvy pet owner may now question whether commercial pet food is safe.

The good news is that most pet food is still safe to feed your dog. Many pet food companies have now put into place quality assurances that have made the pet foods safer. If this is a definite concern to you, the best thing you as a pet owner can do is a bit of research on the foods you intend to feed your dog. Contact the pet food manufacturer directly through their Web site or phone number, and find out if the

━━━━ TIP ━━━━

Is Dry Food Better for Teeth?

It has been thought for some time that dry food is supposedly better for a dog's teeth than canned food, but this is not necessarily the case. Studies have been done that seem to suggest that dry and canned food cause tartar and plaque equally, regardless of their form.

If you want to have food that removes plaque and tartar, you must use a dog food that is formulated as a dental formula. If the food has the logo of the Veterinary Oral Health Center or the American Veterinary Dental College, the food is useful for plaque and tartar control. Otherwise the dog food cannot make such claims.

ingredients go through strict quality control. Does the manufacturer outsource their product or do they have their own factories? Where do they purchase their ingredients?

While this may not totally eliminate the possibility of something dangerous slipping

into the pet food, it will help eliminate those without quality standards and oversight in place. Simply buying from a "trusted brand" is not enough; major manufacturers of pet foods have also been caught up in these quality-control issues.

How to Choose a Dog Food

When you find a dog food that you might want to feed your dog, consider the following before deciding:

• Does it have a statement of nutritional adequacy according to AAFCO (Association of Animal Feed Control Official) guidelines? Not all pet food is labeled as meeting AAFCO standards, so do not assume that the food you are about to feed is. Look at the label.

• Is it a food that is readily available that you can purchase in more than one place? You do not want to be looking all over town for your dog food if your favorite pet boutique no longer carries it or if it is late on Sunday night and they are not open.

• Is it a premium dog food? (More on this later in this chapter.)

• Is the food from a recognizable company with good quality controls and assurances in place?

• Does your dog like to eat it? All the nutrition in the world is worthless if your dog does not like the food and will not eat it.

Premium Dog Food Versus Generic

As a pet owner, you are probably a bit confused over all the dog foods out there. Many are labeled "premium" dog foods, and in truth, there are not going to be too many dog foods that would be labeled "run-of-the-mill" or "generic." After all, who wants to feed that?

The word "premium" has no legal connotation, which makes the term that much more confusing. Any dog food can be called a premium dog food. However, in the context of this book, a premium dog food is one that is characterized by the following attributes:

• It is highly digestible. This means there is less poop to pick up in your yard.

• The protein is based on meat and/or meat by-products, rather than soy, wheat gluten, corn gluten, rice gluten, or bonemeal.

• The meat sources are the first ingredients, rather than grain.

• You feed less because the food is nutrient dense.

• There are no fillers or colors.

Most premium pet foods are available through pet supply stores, but some grocery stores carry them as well. They are expensive when compared to generic dog food, but price and name are not always good indicators. Read the label. Check the manufacturer's Web site for digestibility information.

Why should you care about feeding a premium dog food? First, you will feed less and thereby save money in the long run (you will feed twice to five times as much dog food when it comes to generic foods). Second, because the protein is easier for a dog to digest than many plant proteins, your dog is often getting better nutrition. That shows in his coat, energy level, and muscle tone.

Types of Dog Food: Dry, Canned, Semi-Moist, Frozen, or Freeze-Dried?

The next step is to decide what form of dog food to feed your dog. Most pet foods come in dry or canned versions, but a few come in semi-moist, frozen, or freeze-dried form. The difference between these foods largely has to do with cost and palatability. Let's look at these foods:

• Dry food, or kibble, is the least expensive. Most dog foods come in this form, and it has a shelf life of six months to a year. Negatives: often not as palatable as other forms.

• Canned food is highly palatable. It is the second most common form of dog food, and you can often find the canned version of the same dried premium food. Great for mixing. Good shelf life of a year or more. Negatives: more expensive (you are paying for water) and must feed more in bulk to get the same nutrition as dry.

• Semi-moist food is highly palatable. Originally this food was hamburger-type patties chock-full of preservatives, sugar, and artificial colors—things you do not want to feed your dog. However, recently, compressed meat rolls have appeared on the scene without all the fillers and colors. These are perfectly acceptable as food and treats. Negatives: more expensive to feed. Old-style hamburger-type semi-moist should be avoided because of the sugar, colors, and preservatives.

• Frozen food is highly palatable. Dogs really love this, and as long as it meets AAFCO feeding guidelines, it works well for food. Negatives: expensive and must be kept in the freezer. Danger of bacteria contamination, especially if thawed and refrozen. Must feed more than dry food.

Most people chose to feed either dry kibble or a mixture of these foods.

How to Feed

When your Wheaten is a puppy, you should be feeding him a puppy- or growth-formulated food until he is a year old or until recommended by your veterinarian. After that time, you will need to feed him an adult version of that dog food. Young puppies (younger than six months old) need to be fed three times a day. After six months, you can skip the middle meal and feed twice a day.

When feeding your Wheaten, follow the directions on the package. Because each food

TIP

Switching Dog Foods

Occasionally, you may find it necessary to change dog foods. Perhaps the breeder was feeding one diet, and you wish to feed something else. That is fine, but switching the food over too quickly can cause gastric upsets.

When switching food, you will want to start with a mix of the old food and the new, gradually increasing the amount of new food while decreasing the old food until you completely switch over to the new diet. Most experts recommend the 10-percent rule, that is, each day increase the new dog food by 10 percent and decrease the old dog food by 10 percent until you have completely switched over to the new food. (Use a measuring cup for accuracy.) So, for example, you start with 90 percent old food and 10 percent new food. The next day it is 80 percent old food and 20 percent new food, and so on. If at any time your dog shows diarrhea or other gastric upsets, return to the previous day's portions and feed that. If the gastric upsets continue for more than a day or two, have a veterinarian check your Wheaten to be on the safe side.

has different nutrition and caloric values, there is no one-amount-fits-all among types or brands. Therefore, follow the feeding guidelines first, and then increase or decrease according to your Wheaten's fitness. The total amount for each day should be split into two or three meals, depending on the age of your Wheaten.

In most cases, the amount in the feeding guidelines will be too much and can add unnecessary weight to your Wheaten. This is to ensure that most dogs, regardless of their activity level and metabolism, get enough food. If you find that your Wheaten is looking overweight, cut back the food until he is at the right weight. Continue to feed that amount to maintain that weight.

Free-Feeding

Free-feeding, that is, leaving the food out so your Wheaten can munch on it anytime may be convenient, but it is not necessarily a good idea. Here is why:

• There is no way to monitor how much food your Wheaten eats, thus leading to obesity and other problems.

• If your Wheaten is sick, quite often the first indication is his refusal to eat. You will miss that sign if you free-feed.

• Some behavior problems have been associated with free-feeding. By taking you out of the picture of feeding your dog, your dog does not associate you with the food.

• Food can become rancid or spoiled if left out all day. Mice and bugs can enter and eat the food if left out.

It really does not take much time and effort to fix a dog's food and put down the bowl to feed him. So, consider doing this instead of free-feeding.

Obesity

Obesity is the number-one nutritional problem among pets today; most pets could stand to lose a few pounds. But a few pounds on a Wheaten is not the same as a few pounds on you. A couple of pounds is a lot of weight for a small dog to carry, so it is very important to keep him trim.

You can tell if your Wheaten is obese by placing your thumbs on his spine and feeling his ribs. If you cannot feel his ribs, or if there is a lot of padding between those ribs and your fingers, chances are your dog is overweight and needs to shed some pounds. Have your veterinarian evaluate your dog's weight and suggest a regimen of diet and exercise. There are prescription diets that will help your Wheaten safely lose those added pounds.

Hypoallergenic Diets

One health problem often seen in Wheatens is allergies or intolerances (see Chapter 5 for more on allergies). Because so many allergies are food based, you may want to look for a hypoallergenic diet to feed your Wheaten.

However, before you start changing dog foods, consult with your veterinarian to find out what your Wheaten is really allergic to and to get recommendations on a good hypoallergenic diet. (A lamb and rice mix, contrary to popular belief, is not considered hypoallergenic anymore.)

Treats

Everyone loves to give their dog treats, but unfortunately treats can cause dietary imbalances and can make your Wheaten overweight. Still, if you are training your dog or if you want to reward your Wheaten, treats are often the way to do it.

Limit treats to no more than 5 percent of his total calories. That requires you to look for small, low-calorie treats. Small training biscuits, broken up into several pieces work well, too. So do tiny bits of cooked chicken or beef no bigger than your pinkie nail and tiny bits of carrots or celery, or a dab of plain canned pumpkin.

Avoid feeding your Wheaten "people food" and "table scraps," because quite often they

Dangerous Foods

Here is a list of foods that can be poisonous to your dog. Do not feed them in any quantity. Check the ASPCA Poison Control Center for a list of other dangerous foods (*www.aspca.org*):

- Alcohol (beer, wine, etc.) can lead to alcohol poisoning.
- Chocolate (dark and milk) contains theobromine, which can cause heart, respiratory, gastric, and nervous system problems. Even a small amount of dark chocolate can kill a dog, but milk chocolate can be dangerous, too. (Less than an ounce of dark chocolate can poison a 20-pound dog, and 20 ounces of milk chocolate can kill a 20-pound dog.)
- Coffee contains caffeine, which can act like theobromine.
- Grapes/raisins can cause renal failure.
- Macadamia nuts are poisonous to dogs.
- Onions and garlic can cause hemolytic anemia, a potentially fatal condition where there is an abnormal breakdown of red blood cells and blood vessels.
- Raw salmon contains a fluke that is deadly to dogs.
- Xylitol (artificial sweetener) can send a dog into insulin shock.

are high in fat, sugar, starch, and calories that your Wheaten does not need.

Homemade Diets

With all the concern over commercial pet foods, you may want to feed a homemade diet. Plenty of dogs thrive on homemade diets, but many of these diets are not balanced correctly, and some are downright dangerous. Several popular diets are raw diets that try to mimic a dog's diet in the wild. There are several positives and negatives to a homemade diet. First, the positives:

• You know what is going into your dog's food. You have control over the ingredients.

- It is highly palatable. Dogs love eating these diets.
- It provides a positive interaction between you and your dog.
- You can possibly feed a better diet than what is available commercially.

Now the negatives:

- Many raw diets are contaminated with bacteria such as salmonella, campylobacter, and *E. coli*. This can be mitigated by cooking the food.
- Many diets are not complete and balanced, so you run the risk of causing a serious nutritional deficiency.
- Arguably, bones, both raw and cooked, are considered a hazard, especially if swallowed whole, as they may perforate a dog's intestines. This can be avoided by using ground bone or eggshell.

If you want to feed your dog a homemade diet, you should consult with a veterinary nutritionist over developing an appropriate diet for your Wheaten. There is software available to your veterinarian that will enable him or her to help you balance the food appropriately.

PLE and PLN in Soft Coated Wheaten Terriers

Protein-Losing Enteropathy (PLE) and Protein-Losing Nephropathy (PLN) are two genetic conditions in the Soft Coated Wheaten Terrier. Dogs with these conditions may have skin problems that may otherwise be diagnosed as allergies. Common symptoms

of PLE and PLN are vomiting, diarrhea, decreased appetite, weight loss, fluid retention, and lethargy. Wheatens with PLE/PLN may drink water and urinate excessively. Blood clots form in some Wheatens.

Veterinarians should test any Wheaten that exhibits signs of allergies or PLE/PLN. Wheatens that have this disease should be placed on a gluten-free (no wheat) diet with a novel protein source such as fish, venison, or other protein source not common in dog foods. Lamb is no longer considered a novel protein source because of its prevalence in dog foods. Some Wheatens show sensitivity to chicken, corn, and lamb. If your Wheaten shows any signs of hypersensitivity to such ingredients, your veterinarian can provide you with a hypoallergenic diet. For more on PLE and PLN, see page 57.

GROOMING YOUR SOFT COATED WHEATEN TERRIER

Train Rusty to become used to all the grooming early; it is much harder to train an adult dog later. Get him used to bathing—he will need a bath once a month.

Good Grooming Habits

Soft Coated Wheaten Terriers have single coats and are non-shedding. Their beautiful open coat makes them extremely high-maintenance dogs, requiring constant brushing and combing, on a daily basis in most cases. These fine coats will mat at the slightest opportunity, especially as the Wheaten grows out of his adolescent coat and into his adult coat. The Irish coat needs a little less maintenance compared to the American but still is not a low- or even medium-maintenance coat.

Start learning the proper grooming techniques now. Train Rusty to become used to all the grooming early; it is much harder to train an adult dog later. Teach him to sit or stand quietly on a grooming table while you brush, comb, or trim him. Get him used to bathing—he will need a bath once a month. Obtain the illustrated grooming chart from the Soft Coated Wheaten Terrier Club of America (see address on page 92) and learn what a proper Wheaten trim is.

Even if you decide to use a groomer to bathe and trim your Wheaten—and many Wheaten owners do—you still will have the daunting task of keeping him mat-free and trimmed between grooming visits; otherwise, he will look like an unkempt blond sheepdog.

Grooming Equipment

A word of advice: Do not skimp on equipment. Cheap equipment can break and fall apart and the wrong piece of equipment can ruin the coat. You will need the following

equipment, available from pet supply catalogs or at dog shows:
- Grooming table (arm and noose optional)
- Greyhound comb
- Pin brush
- Slicker brush
- Thinning shears
- Blunt-nosed shears
- Nail trimmers or grinders
- Mat splitter
- Mat rake

- Hair dryer made for dogs (Human hair dryers are too hot for a Wheaten's hair and skin and can scorch.)
- Tweezers or blunt-nosed hemostat
- Styptic powder

When Should You Groom?

Soft Coated Wheaten Terriers require brushing and combing a minimum of three times a week. Adolescent Wheatens between the

ages of twelve and eighteen months may require two or three brushings a day as the adult coat comes in. Wheatens generally need a bath and trimming about once a month. A show Wheaten will need more frequent grooming.

A Show or Pet Trim

Keep your Wheaten in a show or pet trim. An untrimmed Wheaten will become dirty and matted quickly; trimmed Wheatens are easier to care for and will have fewer health problems. If the prospect of trimming your Wheaten seems daunting, most Wheaten breeders will gladly teach you the proper way to trim your Wheaten.

Be certain the groomer knows the proper way to trim a Soft Coated Wheaten Terrier. If he or she does not, find someone who does.

You owe it to the breed to keep your Wheaten in a recognizable cut.

Grooming Your Wheaten

Never trim or bathe a dirty or matted Wheaten. Bathing will cause the mats to worsen; trimming a dirty and matted dog will ruin the trim. Always comb and brush your Wheaten before bathing him and always bathe your Wheaten before trimming him.

Brushing and Combing

Start your brushing and combing session by looking for mats. Wheatens mat easily and you must first remove the mats before brushing and combing. You can remove small mats with the Greyhound comb or mat rake, but the larger mats will require a mat splitter.

Next, brush the hair against the natural lay. Part each layer to the skin and brush back from the skin outward, removing any dead hair and dirt. Do the same with the comb, thoroughly combing out your Wheaten's coat, layer by layer.

Trimming Nails

A Wheaten's toenails are very hard and grow very quickly, so you must trim them weekly. Most Wheatens' toenails are dark, so you may have trouble seeing the "quick" or the blood supply to the nail. When you trim the nail, start cutting a little at a time. If you have let your Wheaten's toenails grow, the quick will be longer. Shortening the nail will cause the quick to recede.

Have styptic powder available in case you do cut the quick. The quick will bleed profusely. Pack the styptic powder into the quick with a cotton ball or ear swab, and the nail will stop bleeding.

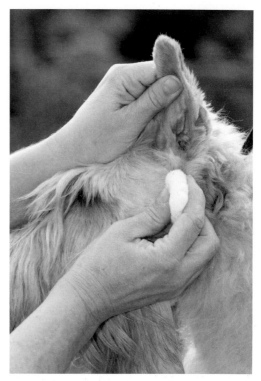

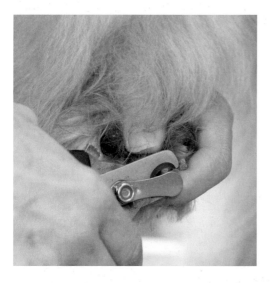

Ears

You should trim around the ears using shears, creating a clean outline. Use your fingers as a guide around the ear to avoid nicking or cutting the earflap. Next, use thinning shears to trim the hair on the ear to give it a natural, layered appearance. The hair should be very short on the tip, gradually becoming longer until it is about three-quarters of an inch at the fold.

Flip the earflap up and use tweezers or hemostats to pluck any hair from the ear canal. If you let the hair grow there, it quickly becomes a place for bacteria and wax to build up. This can cause ear infections.

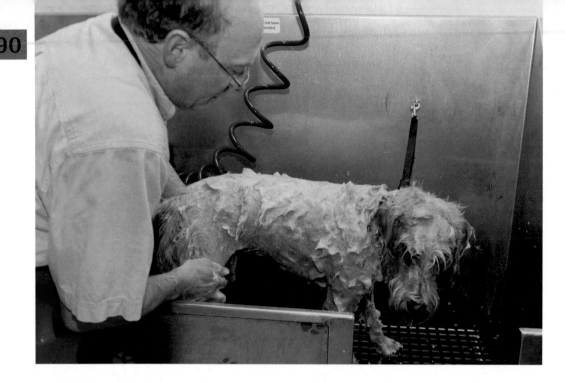

Bathing

Wheatens need a bath about once a month. If you bathe Rusty too often, his skin will become dry. Use a good pH-balanced dog shampoo and conditioner. You can purchase professional dog shampoos and conditioners through pet supply stores and catalogs.

1. Before you bathe, brush, and comb your Wheaten, remove all mats. If he is muddy, allow the mud to dry and comb it out before bathing. Never bathe an uncombed dog.

2. As you wash Rusty, rinse him thoroughly before applying conditioner. Any soap or conditioner in his hair will attract dirt.

3. Apply the conditioner and rinse thoroughly again.

4. Squeeze out excess water from the coat using towels.

5. Brush the coat using a pin brush, while drying the hair.

6. Set the hair dryer to Warm—do not use Hot—and brush out the coat while drying. (Hot dryers can scorch the skin and hair.)

7. Brush the coat against the grain so the dryer's air can dry the coat near the skin. Brush it back so it will lie properly.

Trimming

You can trim your Wheaten any way that suits you, but a shorter trim will be easier to care for. You can keep a shorter trim that reflects the Wheaten's show trim.

Use thinning shears wherever possible to trim. Straight shears will leave scissoring marks in a Wheaten's coat. When you trim, use your grooming table. Train Rusty to stand quietly on the table until you are finished.

Head and neck: The head should be rectangular, smooth, and blended with just a hint of the eye showing. Keep the fall long as it lies over the eyes; you may trim it in a V shape. Cheeks should be flat, not rounded or puffy. Use thinning shears for this. Keep a curved outline around the throat. Make the back of the neck neat with thinning shears.

Legs: Trim the legs with thinning shears to reflect columns. Trim all hair that does not present a clean line. Trim the hair between the pads.

Body: Trim so the Wheaten looks square when standing straight. Trim the belly so there is a proper tuck-up underneath and along the sides. Use thinning shears to blend the hair along the topline for a smooth appearance.

Rear and tail: Trim the rear so that the flank's appearance is neat and blends with the rest of the coat. There should be a tuck-up under the legs. The hip and hock should be defined. Trim the tail so it has a neat appearance. Trim around the anus for hygiene.

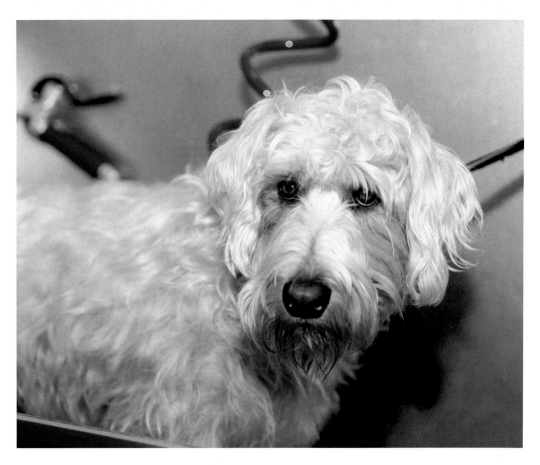

ORGANIZATIONS

American Kennel Club (AKC)
5580 Centerview Drive
Raleigh, NC 27606-3390
Phone: 919-233-9767
Website: *www.akc.org*

AKC Companion Animal Recovery
5580 Centerview Drive, Suite 250
Raleigh, NC 27606-3389
Phone: 1-800-252-7894
Website: *www.akccar.org*

Canine Eye Registration Foundation (CERF)
Department of Veterinary Clinical Science
School of Veterinary Medicine
Purdue University
West Lafayette, IN 47907
Phone: 765-494-8179
Fax: 765-494-9981
Website: *www.vet.purdue.edu/~yshen/
   cerf.html/*

Orthopedic Foundation for Animals (OFA)
2300 Nifong Boulevard
Columbia, MO 65201
Phone: 573-442-0418
Website: *www.offa.org*

PennHIP
Synbiotics Corporation
11011 Via Frontera
San Diego, CA 92127
Phone: 858-451-3771
Fax: 858-451-5719
Website: *www.synbiotics.com/html/
   chdpennhip.html*

Soft Coated Wheaten Terrier Club of America
Website: *www.scwtca.org*

United Kennel Club (UKC)
100 East Kilgore Road
Kalamazoo, MI 49001-5593
Website: *www.ukcdogs.com*

About the Author

Margaret H. Bonham is a multiple award-winning author of more than 30 books and hundreds of articles for magazines such as *Prevention, Dog World, Dog Fancy, Your Dog, Catnip,* and *Mushing Magazine* as well as a content provider for Yahoo!, Ancestry.com, Purina and other websites. She is a world-renown expert in canine and feline behavior. She has been an editor for Howell Book House, Dragon Moon Press, and Wolfsinger Publishing. She is the publisher of Sky Warrior Book Publishing, LLC.

Photo Credits

Barbara Augello: pages 5, 35, 81; Gerry Bucis/Barbara Somerville: page 19; Kent Dannen: pages 6, 7; Tara Darling: pages 63, 83; Cheryl Ertelt: pages 72, 75, 82, 86; Jeanne Pedersen Ferris: pages 4, 9, 11, 12, 14, 15, 16, 17, 20, 25, 27, 28, 36, 54, 61, 65, 67; Daniel Johnson: page 76; Lisa Kruss petphotos.com: page 74; Shutterstock: pages 2, 8, 10, 13, 18, 21, 44, 92, 93; Connie Summers: pages 29, 41, 47, 49, 52, 53, 55, 56, 69, 71, 77, 78, 88, 89 (top), 89 (bottom); Gary Vlahos/Brenmoor: page 48; Joan Hustace Walker: pages 14, 23, 26, 30, 32, 34, 37, 40, 42, 45, 50, 59, 84, 85, 87, 90, 91.

Important Note

This pet owner's guide tells the reader how to buy and care for a Soft Coated Wheaten Terrier. The author and the publisher consider it important to point out that the advice given in the book is meant primarily for normally developed puppies from a good breeder—that is, dogs of excellent physical health and good temperament.

Anyone who adopts a fully grown dog should be aware that the animal has already formed its basic impressions of human beings. There are dogs that as a result of bad experiences with humans behave in an unnatural manner or may even bite. Only people who have experience with dogs should take in such an animal. Even well-behaved and carefully supervised dogs sometimes do damage to someone else's property or cause accidents. It is, therefore, in the owner's interest to be adequately insured against such eventualities, and we strongly urge all dog owners to purchase a liability policy that covers their dog.

Cover Photos

Shutterstock: front cover, back cover, inside front cover, inside back cover.

All inquiries should be addressed to:
Barron's Educational Series, Inc.
250 Wireless Boulevard
Hauppauge, NY 11788
www.barronseduc.com

Library of Congress Catalog Card No. 2011018235

ISBN: 978-0-7641-4612-1

Library of Congress Cataloging-in-Publication Data
Bonham, Margaret H.
   Soft Coated Wheaten Terriers : everything about purchase, care, nutrition, behavior, and training / Margaret H. Bonham. — 2nd ed.
      p. cm. — (Complete pet owner's manual)
      Includes bibliographical references and index.
      ISBN 978-0-7641-4612-1 (pbk.)
   1. Soft coated wheaten terrier. I. Title.
   SF429.S69B66 2011
   636.755--dc23   2011018235

Printed in China
9 8 7 6 5 4 3 2 1